CHAIM BENTORAH

WHAT THE RABBIS KNOW

THAT I NEVER LEARNED IN CHURCH

WHITAKER HOUSE

Unless otherwise indicated, all Scripture quotations are taken from are taken from the King James Version of the Holy Bible. Scripture quotations marked (NKJV) are taken from the New King James Version, © 1982 by Thomas Nelson, Inc. Used by permission. Scripture quotations marked (NLT) are taken from the Holy Bible, New Living Translation, © 1996, 2004, 2015 by Tyndale House Foundation. Used by permission of Tyndale House Publishers, Inc., Carol Stream, Illinois 60188. All rights reserved. Scripture quotations marked (NCV) are taken from the *Holy Bible, New Century Version*®, © 2005 by Thomas Nelson, Inc. Used by permission. All rights reserved. Scripture quotations marked (NIV) are taken from the *Holy Bible, New International Version*®, NIV®, © 1973, 1978, 1984, 2011 by Biblica, Inc. Used with permission. All rights reserved worldwide. Scripture quotations marked (WEB) are taken from the *World English Bible*.

Boldface type in the Scripture quotations indicates the author's emphasis.

WHAT THE RABBIS KNOW THAT I NEVER LEARNED IN CHURCH

www.chaimbentorah.com

ISBN: 979-8-88769-338-5
eBook ISBN: 979-8-88769-339-2
Printed in the United States of America
© 2024 by Chaim Bentorah

Whitaker House
1030 Hunt Valley Circle
New Kensington, PA 15068
www.whitakerhouse.com

Library of Congress Control Number: 2024923353

No part of this book may be reproduced or transmitted in any form or by any means, electronic or mechanical—including photocopying, recording, or by any information storage and retrieval system—without permission in writing from the publisher. Please direct your inquiries to permissionseditor@whitakerhouse.com.

1 2 3 4 5 6 7 8 9 10 11 🕮 32 31 30 29 28 27 26 25

DEDICATION

Rabbi Silverman

Who not only accepted me as a brother but as a spiritual equal.

We will never meet again in this lifetime. But one day, we shall meet again.

TABLE OF CONTENTS

Introduction 11

1. Jewish View on the Inspiration of Scripture 17
2. The Role of the Church 29
3. The High Priest 35
4. Prophets.. 39
5. Scribes... 45
6. Sadducees, Pharisees, and Salvation............................... 49
7. The Gentle One—Nicodemus 55
8. Bind and Loosen... 61
9. The Second Is Like the First 67
10. Where Two or Three Are Gathered 75
11. The Devil.. 79
12. The Nativity... 91
13. The Government Will Be Upon His Shoulders 107

14. The Third Temple 113

15. Transfiguration—Tzim Tzum...................................121

16. Shorten the Way—Kefitzat Haderech 133

17. The Shechinah...139

18. Pardes—A Rabbinical Bible Study Method.............145

19. Washing Your Hands...155

20. Yiredu Our Relationship with Animals...................165

21. The Messiah..173

22. A Jewish Rapture 179

23. Umbilical Cord...189

24. Very Nearly...193

25. The Role of Women..199

26. Capital Punishment...211

27. Gates of Hell...217

28. Forty Days Forty Years...221

29. Jewish Belief About Heaven 231

30. The Inverted Nun...241

31. Evangelism Old Testament Style 247

32. Sarah was a Connection 257

33. Good Wine 265

34. Hosannah..269

35. Where God Dwells...273

36. The Heart of God..279

About the Author...285

Thus saith the LORD of hosts;
In those days it shall come to pass, that ten men shall take
hold out of all languages of the nations, even shall take hold
of the skirt of him that is a Jew, saying,
We will go with you: for we have heard that God is with you.
—Zechariah 8:23 KJV

INTRODUCTION

Many years ago, as a young graduate student, I studied Hebrew under Dr. Earl S. Kalland, who, at that time, was serving on the executive committee doing the translation work on the Old Testament portion of what was to become the New International Version of the Bible. Three times a week, another student and I would sit in Dr. Kalland's office, and he would discuss his work on the New International Version of the Bible with us while waiting for us to challenge him on some of his renderings from the original Hebrew.

One day, we discussed Psalm 25:14: "*The secret of the LORD is with them that fear him.*" Dr. Kalland advised us that it was agreed they would render this as "*The LORD confides in those who fear him*" (NIV). Having my undergraduate degree in Jewish studies, I strongly objected. I explained to Dr. Kalland that the word *sod*, which is rendered as secret, has a much more profound emotional understanding to Jewish rabbis than just a mere confiding. Dr. Kalland was intrigued and suggested I search out an orthodox

12 *What the Rabbis Know That I Never Learned in Church*

rabbi and discuss with him why the word *sod* has such an emotional effect.

I found such a rabbi but discovered he was more interested in the idea of a new major English translation of the Bible than discussing the word *sod*. Now, however, years later, I realize he was answering my question about the word *sod*.

To answer his questions on a modern translation of the Bible, I explained to him how specific passages of Scripture from the Old Testament were sent to Hebrew scholars throughout the world who would study these passages from the original Hebrew and then send their suggested translation of the passage to a committee that would decide on what was to be included in the final version.

The rabbi looked at me quizzically and asked: "Do you mean to tell me that just a handful of academics will tell millions of Christians what the Holy Scriptures really say?" Unlike the Jews, we Christians do not teach our children to study the Word of God in the original language as they do. We have no choice but to depend upon a handful of scholars to decide how certain words in Hebrew should be described. I soon learned that rabbis do not trust English translations of the Torah and use them sparingly. They prefer to study the Torah from the original Hebrew to decide what a particular word means. They feel the Holy Spirit can speak to them personally from the Word of God without the benefit of a translator.

So, I just shrugged and told the rabbi that most Christians depend upon a handful of scholars to tell us what the Holy Scriptures teach and confided we do not take a study of the original languages as seriously as the Jews do.

He then asked me what the word for "learning" was in Hebrew. I told him it was *lamed* like the letter Lamed. He agreed and added that the word also began with the letter Lamed. He then asked what the word for a king was, and I said it was *melek*. The rabbi also agreed and added that this word began with a Mem. He then asked which letter came first in the Hebrew alphabet, the Lamed or the Mem. I told him it was like our English alphabet; Lamed is the letter L and comes before the Mem, which is the letter M. The rabbi then leaned back in his chair and said, "These Hebrew scholars, they have set themselves up as kings to rule over the Christian's understanding of the Holy Scriptures, do they not?" I had to agree that, in a sense, he was right.

The rabbi leaned forward and said, "You put the Lamed, your learning from the *Ruach Hakodesh* (Holy Spirit), before the Mem, the kings; you are following the right order. But if you put the Mem before the Lamed—the kings before the learning—you receive from the *Ruach Hakodesh*, you are totally out of order and must beware."

I had never experienced any of my Christian Hebrew teachers using the Hebrew language like this rabbi, and I was soon to learn how other rabbis used Hebrew. I began to realize that the biblical Hebrew language, to a rabbi, was something sacred and holy. They are very cautious in their use of Hebrew but paradoxically very free to do things with the Hebrew language that my Christian Hebrew teachers would never think of doing. Rabbis were familiar with finding relationships between words that have the same numerical value, rearranging the letters in a Hebrew word to discover some deeper understanding, searching for word plays, finding deeper meanings and hidden meanings in loan words for other Semitic languages, and tracing words to their etymological roots.

For example, we come across verses like Exodus 32:10–11, 14:

Now therefore let me alone, that my wrath may wax hot against them, and that I may consume them: and I will make of thee a great nation. And Moses besought the LORD *his God, and said,* LORD, *why doth thy wrath wax hot against thy people, which thou hast brought forth out of the land of Egypt*

14 *What the Rabbis Know That I Never Learned in Church*

with great power, and with a mighty hand? … And the LORD *repented of the evil which he thought to do unto his people.*

We see the word *"wrath"* or *"anger"* as found in other modern translations and picture a God seething with rage, ready to act irrationally. Then Moses attempts to calm God down: "God, You're upset; You don't know what You're saying. Now calm down, count to ten—Aleph, Beth, Gimmel. Here, have a piece of bagel; You'll feel better." Then, when Moses settled God down and explained how God's threats would backfire on Him, God finally cooled down and said, "Moses, when you're right, you're right. I don't know what came over Me; of course, I will not do this evil to the people I threaten to do." This whole passage and the anger of God never made any sense to me. Here, we have a God who is ready to destroy His own people for some infraction of His rules, and it takes one of His created beings to cool Him down and explain the illogical and irrational behavior of God. Such behavior would strike fear in anyone who is under the dominion of an omnipotent God capable of losing all control. How do you justify a verse like 1 John 4:18? *"There is no fear in love; but perfect love casteth out fear: because fear hath torment. He that feareth is not made perfect in love."* If God is perfect in love, how can He strike such fear in us?

I asked a rabbi once about this passage, and he asked me to trace the origin of the word for "wrath" or "anger." When I did, I found it was the word *aph* from the root word *aneph*. This word is an onomatopoeia, which mimics the sounds or noises they refer to. For instance, the word "woof" sounds like the bark of a dog. *Aneph* mimics the sound of the snort of a camel. I realized I needed to move beyond my lexicon and research the habits of camels as the word *aneph*, which we so easily apply the English word anger to, is rooted in a simple Bedouin's observation of his camel. I learned a camel will snort when angry or upset, but it will also snort when forced to do something it does not want to do. It will snort when it is grieving, such as when its mate or its owner dies. It will also snort when in heat or when it desires intimacy with another camel.

I now understand what the rabbi meant by putting the Lamed, the learning from the Holy Spirit, before the teaching of the Mem or kings. The kings tell me that God is an angry God who is ready to squish us like a bug if we step out of line. Deep within my spirit, I sense the Spirit of God saying, "Have you considered that maybe God was not angry but grieving? Have you considered that God possibly longs and desires an intimate relationship with us so much that His desire for intimacy with us burns such that He must turn away from us because our sin makes it impossible for a pure and holy God to be intimate with us?"

What profoundly impacted me was that in the forty years since my interview with this rabbi, I have never read in Jewish literature nor heard another rabbi talk about the Lamed and the Mem and putting the learning of the Holy Spirit before the king. In fact, after forty years of studying the works of rabbis, I have learned that original thinking is respected and cherished by the Jews. God is, after all, an infinite God. If He is infinite, then there must not be an end to the wisdom and knowledge of God. After hundreds of years of original expression in the arts, a new song, melody, poem, and story are being written every day. Indeed, after the hundreds and thousands of songs that have been written, it might seem like we have reached the end of the possibility of a new song or a new melody. Still, something new is always hitting our markets.

Yet, within Christianity, we act as if all that can be said about the Word of God has been said. There seems to be no room for original thinking or new insights into the Word of God. We must always quote from some ancient source rather than use that ancient source as a guide to another chamber into the heart of God. If no two snowflakes are alike, if no two people are perfectly identical in appearance and personality out of the billions who have walked this earth, could not an infinite God relate to each person uniquely and specially?

Rabbis have taught me that there is always room for new insights. I recall a rabbi telling me that when he was attending a yeshiva, he recalled studying the Torah with his study partner. After a few hours of study, the elderly and learned rabbi would sit down with them and ask, "What can you teach me? What can I learn from you?"

Let me share with you some of the things I have learned from the rabbis, which are totally out of the Christian box, yet you will not be leaving your Christian faith.

1

JEWISH VIEW ON THE INSPIRATION OF SCRIPTURE

In Christianity we hear vague references from the Jewish people to works such as the Talmud, the Midrash, or the Kabbalah. I recall that Judaism was one of the religions we studied in a comparative religion class at Bible college. My professor indicated that one of the holy books was the Talmud, which was "just" a compilation of various rabbis' opinions on what other rabbis have said. He then said that the Jews held these writings up as inspired, almost like the Bible itself—at least he said "almost."

To be fair to my former professor, whom I highly respected, I understand what he was trying to say. This matter of inspiration of Scripture is a very complex issue for the Jewish people. Yet, thanks to my struggle with what they believed about the Scriptures and their holy books, I have come to understand my position on the inspiration of the Bible and to appreciate the Word of God more than I ever had within my Christian faith.

I rarely hear the term "inspiration of Scripture" used among Jews. What they speak about is the *divinity* of Scripture. Christians

18 *What the Rabbis Know That I Never Learned in Church*

put Scripture into one neat package that we call the Bible, which includes the thirty-nine books of the Old Testament and the twenty-seven books of the New Testament. We draw upon the statement of the Apostle Paul in 2 Timothy 3:16: *"All scripture is given by inspiration of God, and is profitable for doctrine, for reproof, for correction, for instruction in righteousness."* From this, we in Christianity conclude that the Bible is the very Word of God. However, there is much debate over what Scripture is and what it means to be inspired.

I consider myself a part of the evangelical community, which believes that the thirty-nine books of the Old Testament and twenty-seven books of the New Testament are divinely inspired without error. However, there are those in Christianity who believe there are eighty books of the Bible, which include another fourteen books in the Apocrypha, which are additional writings not forming a part of the accepted canon of Scripture. The biblical canon consists of a set of books that are accepted as the inspired Word of God. Initially, the apocryphal books were considered edifying but not divinely inspired, so they were read privately but not in the public context of church services. Later, after the Reformation, the Protestant churches redefined the Apocrypha as heresy.

The Jewish Bible, often referred to as the Hebrew Bible or the Tanakh, and even in specific contexts, the Torah, has twenty-four books divided into three parts. The first five books of the Bible are called the Torah, which means teachings. Then there are the eight books of the *Nevi'im* or the prophet and the eleven books called the *Ketuvim* or writings, written in Hebrew with some portions in the Chaldean dialect of Aramaic. The Protestant Bible divided these twenty-four books into thirty-nine books, so the content of the Tanakh is the same as the Old Testament of our Protestant Bible.

When the apostle Paul wrote 2 Timothy 3:16, calling all Scripture inspired by God, he was referred to the twenty-four books of the Jewish Hebrew Bible (thirty-nine books in the Protestant Old Testament) as the Scriptures. The word "Scripture" in Greek is *graphe*, which means writings. In Aramaic, it is the word *katav*, which also means writings or books. This could include many of the apocryphal books that were available at this time. Contextually, however, we in the evangelical community believe Paul was referencing just the specific twenty-four books of the Jewish Bible, which the Jews canonized at this time.

In this sense, canonization would mean those books were considered divine or divinely inspired in our Christian understanding. The word "inspiration" in Greek is *theopneustos*, which means God-breathed (*theos*—God, *pneuma*—breath/spirit). In the Aramaic the word used is *davarucha*, which refers to words from the heart (of God).

Technically, we evangelical Christians are on the same page as the Jews concerning the Old Testament as the inspired, divine work of God. Judaism and Christianity are subject to many theories regarding how these words from the heart of God made it into the written Word and what it means to be genuinely inspired by God.

There are at least seven viewpoints on the authority of Scripture, which can be found among many Jews.

1. The intuition theory: This theory is also known as the illumination theory, which teaches that the writings of Scripture are not inspired, but it is the writers God inspired as to what to write.

2. The dynamic theory: This is also known as the partial inspiration theory, which teaches that God enabled the writer to receive the transmission of the words of His heart. Thus, the writers were infallible only in matters of faith and practice but not necessarily in their non-religious issues. This concludes that only portions of

Scripture, like prophetic passages, are inspired. Phrases like "and these are the travels of the children of Israel" would be added by the writer but would not be considered part of the divine revelation from God.

3. The neo-orthodox inspiration theory: This view maintains that there may be supernatural elements present in Scripture, but like any literary work, the Bible still contains errors, and not all events in the Bible should be taken literally. Truth is realized only through the individual who will recognize or comprehend it. In other words, the Bible itself is not divinely inspired but only serves as a channel through which the divine inspiration will flow. Truth is left to the discretion of the individual.

4. The natural inspiration theory: This view says there is nothing supernatural about the Bible; writers wrote it through human inspiration based on their own experiences and biases. It is no different than the inspiration of a classic writer like Charles Dickens or Ernest Hemingway. Unlike the intuition theory, God plays no role in the inspiration behind the writing.

5. The conceptual inspiration theory: In this theory, the thoughts of Scripture are inspired but not the actual words. Only the concepts or thoughts in the Bible are inspired. In other words, God gave the writer the ideas, which the writer put into their own words.

6. The dictation theory: This turns the writer into a dictation or recording machine. It's sort of like a stenographer or a court reporter who records what they hear word for word. No individual personality or writing style is expressed. The writer was no more than a recording device.

7. The verbal, plenary inspiration theory: This is the view that I hold. The Holy Spirit provided the verbal, plenary, and complete knowledge that God wished to express—verbal being the words or ideas of Scripture. God directed the choice of the individual words in the original Greek, Hebrew, or Aramaic language that the writers used in the original manuscripts. However, God used the unique backgrounds and personalities of the writers to create the written document in their writing style. The Holy Spirit directed the writers so that the original manuscripts were infallible and without error.

For the most part, religious Jews believe that God inspired the Old Testament or Tanakh, but their understanding of inspiration is as varied as that in the Christian realm. The difference might lie in the fact that for a Christian, only one of the seven theories of inspiration would apply to the entirety of Scripture. In contrast, some Jews might view the first five books or Torah as inspired according to the last three theories of inspiration and the remaining books as being inspired according to the first four theories. I believe this is why they avoid using the word "inspiration," as there are many different ideas about what inspiration means and various levels of inspiration. It is much simpler to say that the Tanakh is of divine origin or that the first five books are more of a divine origin than the remainder of the Tanakh, as God gave the first five books verbally on Mt. Sinai where they were recorded by Moses. Unlike Christianity, which would hold to just one view of the inspiration of Scripture, many Jews believe the first five books of the Bible were more divine than the remaining books. The Torah, or the first five books would be more divinely inspired than the remaining. Although they would view different levels of inspiration, and some books were more inspired than others, the Jews still believed that the Old Testament or Tanakh was of divine origin. They honored the entire Tanakh as truly the Word of God.

22 *What the Rabbis Know That I Never Learned in Church*

The other works that are considered sacred, such as the Talmud, Midrash, and Kabbalah, are not considered to be of divine origin but are sacred because they do bear the *shemot,* that is, writings that include the name of God. Any works that include the name of God are considered sacred, and there are all sorts of *halachas,* that is, Jewish religious laws regarding their disposal. This would consist of books that serve as a commentary or explanation of the Torah. Although considered sacred, they are not regarded as authoritative as the Torah or Tanakh.

Christians might hold a similar view about biblical commentaries or Bible handbooks. An exception would be that they are considered sacred for the very reason that they contain the name of God. I do not find the works of Rashi, a medieval Jewish commentator, and Hebrew master, much different from modern study Bibles. Rashi's historical, cultural, and linguistic comments on the Hebrew Bible are similar to those of our contemporary Christian commentators, who are found alongside the scriptural text in study Bibles.

The following list highlights some of the major works or writings of Jewish teachers referenced in this text:

1. The Talmud: This is the central text of rabbinic literature and the primary source of Jewish religious law and theology. The main collection of writings is in the Babylonian Talmud (Talmud Bavli), compiled in the fifth century AD. An earlier collection was known as the Jerusalem Talmud (Talmud Yerushalmi). The Talmud has two components. The first component is the Mishnah, which compiles the teachings prior to the first century AD in a written form. Before this, these teachings were oral traditions or what the New Testament called the tradition of the fathers [elders] (see Matthew 15:2 and Mark 7:5). The second component is the Gemara, which clarifies the Mishnah, which

is a commentary on the commentary. The Babylonian Talmud can be found in thirty to thirty-five volumes and is written in Aramaic and Hebrew. The Jerusalem Talmud has about seventeen volumes and is also written in Aramaic and Hebrew, although the Aramaic is a Northern Aramaic dialect.

I have found the Talmud to be an excellent resource for helping to understand many references in the New Testament as it reflects Jewish thought on theology and teachings during the first century. As oral tradition or the tradition of the fathers was studied during the first century during the time of Jesus, and He made many references to these teachings as later recorded in the Talmud. As you will find in this book, the Talmud sheds a significant light on understanding many of the teachings found in the New Testament.

2. The Midrash: Midrash means textual interpretation and is a multi-volume study of Jewish Biblical exegesis (critical explanation and interpretation). These works involve questions and various answers surrounding biblical texts. Often, stories from the Torah are reimagined to stand alongside, not to replace, scriptural references. An example would be the story of Hagar, who was banished by Abraham's wife Sarah. (See Genesis 16.) The Midrash expands this story by teaching that Hagar is Keturah, who married Abraham after Sarah died. Isaac sought out Hagar/Keturah to return and be Abraham's wife after the passing of his mother, Sarah. This is to show Isaac's devotion and caring nature. Although this is not explicitly stated in the Torah, it is used to help give a deeper understanding of the characters of Isaac and Abraham.

24   *What the Rabbis Know That I Never Learned in Church*

3. The Targum: The Targum is an Aramaic translation of the Torah that was translated during the time of Jesus and the apostle Paul. It was translated as a paraphrase and thus was not accepted initially as authoritative as the Hebrew Scriptures, but it helps understand Jewish thought in the first century.

4. Kabbalah: This is a book on Jewish mysticism. The definition of Kabbalah can vary according to tradition and the goals of those who follow it. It developed during medieval times and consisted of esoteric teachings meant to explain the relationship between God and the natural world. The Zohar is the foundational work of the Kabbalah, which includes a commentary on the mystical aspects of the Torah. It discusses the nature of God, the nature of souls, redemption, and the relationship between darkness and light.

   Although "mysticism" may be a forbidden word among evangelical Christians, much of Jewish mysticism only teaches that a supernatural God desires a personal relationship with the human beings that He created and that such a relationship is possible. Jewish mystics are those who believe that God does hear and answer our prayers and that He does speak to us just as we may talk to Him. This is a simplistic explanation of Jewish mysticism; by that definition, we should have no problems with Jewish mysticism. You may find my chapter on the *tzim tzum*, which is very mystical—that is, mystical in the sense of a relationship with God—to be quite interesting and helpful in understanding such things as the transfiguration and Paul's experience on the Damascus Road.

   There is an old German proverb translated by Thomas Carlyle and used by George Bernard Shaw in several of his books: "We are apt to make the usual blunder of emptying the baby of the bath." Today we say, "Don't throw the baby out with the bath water." Much of what you will find in Jewish mysticism is just bath water, but if you don't throw the baby out, it could grow into a real spiritual blessing to your Christian faith.

Concerning the Jewish position on the Scriptures as of divine origin, I found that my struggles through my academic training and research on the Bible caused me to question the authority of Scripture. My experience with rabbis and their love for the Holy Scriptures from reformed to conservative to orthodox has given me a new love and respect for the Word of God and reinforced my belief that every word of the Bible is God-breathed.

I am not impressed with historical proofs that use logic to claim the Bible is indeed the Word of God. Some Bible teachers try to use the odds of the prophecies that have been fulfilled to show definitive proof that the Bible is divinely inspired. What is impressive is how the Jews treat the Torah, rejoice over the Torah, honor the Torah, and love the Torah. Any commentary or writing with the name of God is considered sacred and treated with respect. I realized that the bottom line is the Bible is a book about God, and I believe in God. It stands to reason that this God who desires so much for a relationship with me would not give me a book that tells me all I need to know to have that relationship, but instead points me toward the Source. I must seek Him out and cultivate that connection.

By faith, I accept the Bible that I carry is the infallible, inspired, and inerrant Word of God. The love of the Torah I find among the rabbis has strengthened my faith in the Word of God and causes me to give prayerful consideration to any commentary written to honor the name of God, even if the authors' theology or doctrine is not accepted in my camp.

I was on a business trip to California many years ago, and my plane had a three-hour Sunday morning layover in Denver. As I sat in the Denver airport, waiting for my connection, I heard an announcement that a Catholic mass would be offered in the airport chapel. I am not Catholic, but it was my Sabbath day, and I figured it was something Christian, so I decided to attend this mass. As it turned out, it was not a mass because the facilitator was just a deacon and not an ordained priest, so he could not offer communion. However, he did offer a reading of the liturgy, which included the Word of God and some commentary. As I sat through this service with about fifteen other worshippers, I began to weep when I heard the name of God and His Word spoken. I noticed not many dry eyes from the other travelers who paused in their journey to worship the God I loved. After the service ended, I shook the deacon's hand and asked if this wonderful feeling of God's presence was always like this in the little chapel. He said with tears still in his eyes: "No, this is the first time."

Not only did I feel the presence of God, but I believe I also felt the presence of old Jewish rabbis and Jewish patriarchs such as Abraham, Isaac, and Jacob, who said: "Don't get hung up on definitions and nuances, just accept that book that you have in your hands as the Word of God and love it as we do."

> *All scripture is given by inspiration of God, and is profitable for doctrine, for reproof, for correction, for instruction in righteousness.* (2 Timothy 3:16)

Not only have the rabbis instilled in me a love for the Word of God but also a burning desire to study the Word of God in depth and come to an original or personal understanding of Scripture rather than a sense of how Scripture relates to my particular denomination and theological persuasion. I learned not to depend upon my favorite teacher or preacher to guide me to understand Scripture but to study the Word of God and allow the Holy Spirit

Jewish View on the Inspiration of Scripture   27

to be my teacher. I learned to respect the interpretation of Scripture from other teachers and to realize that there are seventy faces of the Torah. The Word of God is like a gem; you see many colors when you allow the light to shine through it. I finally learned that the Word of God is a well that will never run dry and that a verse of Scripture that had a specific meaning for me as a child took on a deeper meaning as I matured in my relationship with God. The older I grow in my relationship with God, the deeper and richer my understanding of particular passages of Scripture becomes.

Rabbis have taught me that even though the Word of God is inspired, it has many layers of understanding. It is a miracle that humanity has a book that speaks to us all; it transcends thousands of years, thousands of cultures, and has been translated into many different languages. I am not in a position to explain the theological understanding of the inspiration of Scripture, but I believe it addresses every human being no matter where or when they lived.

I find myself drawn to the teachings of Jewish teachers. The first Christians were Jews; most of the Bible is about the Jewish people, their culture, and history. The Jews are people of the Hebrew language and the masters of this language that the Old Testament was written in. So why not study their commentaries and their understandings of the Holy Scriptures? No rabbis subscribe to my Baptist doctrine, but we share the same God, love the same God, and worship the same God. If I spend my time studying the works of those who subscribe to my particular Protestant denomination and theology, I will limit myself from knowledge and wisdom that existed long before the first Baptist walked this earth. To read the works of Jewish teachers who lived long before the Christian faith appeared on this planet is to examine the roots of my faith in God. In discovering my roots in the Jewish faith, I find myself even more firmly planted in my Christian faith as it relates to me personally and culturally. The same Holy Spirit that led the fathers of Judaism is the same Holy Spirit that leads me and teaches me.

My brother is a linguist who translated the Bible into the Amanab language in Papua New Guinea. These villagers had no concept of a lamb, sheep, or shepherd. Psalm 23's speaking of the Lord as our Shepherd created quite a challenge for my brother. Yet, the Bible was written by God for that villager living in a primitive culture who has no concept of sheep, and just as much for me as for the Middle Eastern shepherd, and Psalm 23 speaks to the heart of that primitive villager just as it speaks to me as it would to a Middle Eastern shepherd.

One night, as my brother and one of the villagers sat out under the stars just talking, this villager said: "Andy, long before you came to our village, I looked up at the stars and prayed to your God to send someone to teach us about Him, and then you came and you not only came to teach us but to give us His Word in our language."

There is no way you can explain what the inspiration of Scripture means to this villager other than that it is the Word of God, and he loves it. There is no way to teach this villager to adjust to the strange culture that my brother came from, where we know about sheep and shepherds, but he can still teach those villagers about God because the Holy Spirit will bring them understanding.

Although I am not Jewish and I am not part of their culture, Judaism still taught me that the Word of God, the Bible as we Christians call it, is truly a divine book. This book tells us what God wants us to know and embrace. I have no fear of studying their works because my teacher is the Holy Spirit.

2

THE ROLE OF THE CHURCH

The role of the church is directly tied to the Scripture. We Christians tend to think of the synagogue as a Jewish church. In many respects, this is not true. However, it is true in the role of Scripture. First, let me explain the origin of the Synagogue.

Scripture teaches that the twelve tribes of Israel introduced the twelve family groups that grew out from the twelve sons of Jacob. When the twelve tribes of Israel entered the promised land, each tribe was given a territory of land to farm and raise their families. However, no land was given to the tribe of Levi; their portion or inheritance was dedicated to the Lord. They devoted their lives to studying the Torah and serving God. Their support came from the other eleven tribes. They were the priestly tribe who handled the spiritual affairs of the rest of the nation. Their service centered around the tabernacle and, eventually, the temple. They were supported by a tithe, which means a tenth. Each tribe gave ten percent of their produce to support the tribe of Levi, which had no other way to support themselves.

The tithe was only meant to be given to the priestly tribe of Israel so they could perform their duties within the tabernacle and later the temple, and other priestly duties. When the temple was destroyed, the purpose of the tithe no longer existed. I had one rabbi tell me that he would consider it a sin if his congregation tithed. Offerings are accepted to help the needy, but the synagogue is not a temple, and there is no command to support the synagogue with a tithe. The synagogue is supported through the payment of dues like a membership fee, and it is out of this that the rabbi receives his salary. He is not a priest so he does not accept a tithe. A rabbi is not paid to be a rabbi; like an employee, he is paid so he does not have to do anything but serve as a rabbi.

It is for this reason that I do not tithe, nor do I accept tithes in my ministry. I do give offerings, but I do not limit myself to ten percent. I consider everything I have to belong to God, and I give an offering as I feel led by God. I am not advocating that pastors remove the word "tithe" from their vocabulary. My choice to do so is the result of the influence of Judaism in my life.

Before the destruction of the second temple in 70 AD, a group of religious leaders who were not really part of the tribe of Levi arose who devoted themselves to the study and teaching of the Torah. They were called Pharisees, Sadducees, and scribes. They were a non-professional religious sect. Their role could be compared to the non-priestly religious orders within the Catholic church like the Benedictines, the Carmelites, and the Franciscans. In the Catholic church, the members of these orders are not priests nor do they perform the role of a priest, although a male can pursue that role and still be a member of their order.

With the temple's destruction, the synagogue became the center for worship and learning, and without the need for a priestly office, many non-Levites assumed the role of the teachers. The Pharisees were the most logical ones to assume the role of the teachers, or rabbis, as they were usually the most learned in the study of the Torah. Foremost in the synagogues was the Torah. The Word of God was front and center, and the Pharisees devoted their lives to the study of Torah and its preservation, and eventually became known as rabbis.

The synagogue is sometimes referred to as a *shul*. Shul is an old German word for a place of learning. It is a place of worship, but worship in the sense of being a house of prayer. This takes place in the main sanctuary. The main sanctuary may also be used for special ceremonies such as weddings and on rare occasions funerals, although the casket is not allowed in the sanctuary. The synagogue is often referred to as a *Beyt Knesset* (House of Assembly) or *Beyt Tefillah* (House of Prayer). There is also a separate place of learning, called a midrash room.

In the Christian church, the focus of the sanctuary is the pulpit, where the preacher teaches from and about the Holy Scriptures. The focus in the Synagogue is not a pulpit or *bimah* as it is called, but the ark, which contains the *Sefer Torah* or the Torah Scrolls. This is the first thing that struck me as the difference between Judaism and Christianity. The Word of God is front and center in Judaism and not the rabbi. The Torah Scrolls are kept in an ark, a sort of closet where it is covered with multiple coverings referred to as a mantel. The idea is that a valuable treasure is not left exposed and vulnerable. The Torah Scrolls are not worshipped but are respected and honored.

The *bimah* is a table where the Torah Scrolls are opened to be read. The rabbi does preach a simple sermon from the Torah; however, it is usually much more subdued than the sermons of many preachers who seek to be very dramatic in their delivery.

The rabbi, unlike what we find in Christianity, has not been given any special status or authority to conduct religious services. Any Jew with sufficient education to know what he is doing can lead a religious service. That may be true in many sectors of Christianity if an ordained preacher is not available. However, we

32 *What the Rabbis Know That I Never Learned in Church*

just don't have the feeling that the service rendered by the layman is as valid as a genuine ordained preacher. It is rare that a church is without a pastor or preacher, while it is not unusual for a community to be without a rabbi.

The impression I received was that the rabbi did not seek to take center stage. Nor have I met any rabbis who seem to take themselves too seriously. There is a greater emphasis on the Torah, and all respect and honor is directed to the Word of God. The rabbi seems to be more of a facilitator. After experiencing a Jewish worship service, I found myself to be very sensitive to church services where the preacher or pastor is given a place of honor, and stands on a raised platform, psychologically placing himself above the members of the congregation, oftentimes wearing beautiful robes or expensive business suits. More and more preachers do not stand behind a pulpit or podium, which is fine with me. However, it seems with the introduction of modern technology, Scripture passages are projected on a screen, and the preacher has no need for a pulpit or podium on which to place his Bible. They often do not have a Bible in their hands. Traditionally, the pulpit was considered sacred because that is where the preacher placed his Bible, the Word of God, which was traditionally the focus of the worship service. The preacher is almost idolized in many churches; he is considered a man of God who is somehow closer to God, and hence, if you need prayer, you go to the preacher as you somehow feel his prayers are more effective than those of your own loved ones.

I find many preachers take themselves a little too seriously. They acquire and cherish the title of reverend, and many Christian colleges and universities offer a doctor of ministry degree, which basically requires a few years of religious service and a paper on some religious topic and you have the privilege of not only being called Rev. So and So but Dr. So and So, making them more distinguished. Many rabbis have advanced degrees and doctorates but prefer not to be referred to as doctor. They are satisfied with just the title of rabbi, which does not make them any more distinguished from their peers despite having advanced academic degrees where others may not. Without the use of honorifics, we are reminded that we each have the same amount of the Holy Spirit as the next believer, and it is the Holy Spirit that is our true teacher.

3

THE HIGH PRIEST

"For we have not an high priest which cannot be touched with the feeling of our infirmities; but was in all points tempted like as we are, yet without sin."
—Hebrews 4:15

I have often wondered why Paul pictures Jesus as a High Priest who understands our infirmities. I found an answer to that when I took a dive into Jewish history and culture.

In Judaism, the office of the high priest ended with the destruction of the second temple in 70 AD. For us Christians, it ended with the death and resurrection of Jesus, who became our High Priest. Have you ever wondered what Jesus as our High Priest means? High priest in Aramaic in reference to Jesus is *rabkumra*, which is translated as high priest but is made up of the words *rab*, where we get rabbi, which means master or chief, and *kumra*, which is from the root word *kamar*, which has the idea of shrinkage or humility. The Hebrew word for high priest is *kohan gadol*, the great or chief priest. The word in the Greek is *archierea*. You may recognize the prefix "arch," which means the chief (priest).

Here is what I find interesting in Aramaic. The Aramaic word used in the Gospels for high priest is simply *raba*, which is the word for rabbi. It does not include the word *kumra*. But kumra is attached to the role Jesus played. The role of Jesus is not just that of the High Priest but the High Priest who is humble and has lowered Himself. You see, Jesus is the Son of God; to be a High Priest in terms of rank on a heavenly level is pretty low, lower than the angels. To be our Savior, however, He had to lower Himself to the rank of High Priest. He had to take a demotion, *kumra*, and shrink down to the level of a human to assume the position of High Priest.

But why a high priest? I did some checking in the Talmud and discovered some amazing things. For one thing, as we all know, only the high priest is allowed to enter the holy of holies on the Day of Atonement when he offers a sacrifice for the sin of all the people. He literally takes on the sins of the entire nation as Jesus took on the sins of the entire world. But here is something you may not know. In the Talmud, Yoma 18a says that the high priest had to be rich. If he were not a man of wealth when he assumed the office, it was up to the other priest to make sure he was rich. He had to be superior to everyone in his wealth. But not only in his wealth but his physique, wisdom, and dignity. Remember Luke 2:52: "*And Jesus increased in wisdom and stature, and in favour with God and man.*" That is exactly the requirement laid down in the Talmud for a high priest. Although Jesus was not materially wealthy, He was superior in wealth in a spiritual sense. He also had to be married and married to only one woman. If his wife were to die before the Day of Atonement, the high priest had to remarry before he could offer the sacrifice on Yom Kippur. The high priest had to be married so he could relate and understand the dynamics of an intimate relationship with one person and understand the

The High Priest 37

commitment and faithfulness to one individual. My study partner explained to me how this relates to our High Priest, Jesus. Jesus, as our High Priest, is married to us. For the high priest to be married, it meant he had to share his heart with his wife and make himself vulnerable to her, like every man does with his wife when he gives her his heart. He gives her the ability to break his heart just as Jesus makes Himself vulnerable to us when He gives us His heart. Perhaps that is why God is near to the brokenhearted as we learn in Psalm 34:18. He understands a broken heart, for we have broken His heart many times when we pursue other gods.

There is something else I found strange about the high priest in the Talmud. This is found in Sanhedrin 18a. Here we read that the wife of the high priest had the right to divorce her husband, and if she did, she would be allowed to marry another man. In the Hebrew culture, only the man had the right to divorce; a woman could not get a divorce unless there was a very special circumstance. Again, my study partner pointed out that this shows God's loyalty to us. He will never divorce us once we are married to Him. We can divorce Him and marry ourselves to other gods, but God will also remain faithful to us.

> Thus saith the LORD, Where is the bill of your mother's divorcement, whom I have put away? or which of my creditors is it to whom I have sold you? Behold, for your iniquities have ye sold yourselves, and for your transgressions is your mother put away. (Isaiah 50:1)

There is one more thing, however, I would like to share. In the Talmud, Sanhedrin 4a, we find that a high priest cannot be seen disrobed or naked. This would occur when washing in the *mikveh* partial bathing or the *tevilah* entire immersion. This was often not a private bath but a shared bath. Public bathhouses were quite common and even exist today in many cultues. Not everyone had a private bath in those days except for the high priest.

Now, here is the strange thing about this arrangement. Although much caution would be made to make sure the high priest was not seen naked, the high priest himself could invite anyone he wants to share a bath with him.

So, what is the parallel of this to our *Rabkumra* High Priest Jesus? My study partner was able to provide an explanation that was thought provoking. This is again a picture of entering the heart of Jesus. *"Many are called, but few are chosen"* (Matthew 22:14). Many are born again but not all are invited to share the intimacy of a *tevilah* with Jesus. That is, not everyone seeks to develop their relationship with Jesus on a daily basis in prayer and Bible study, where they become such friends with Jesus that He will trust them enough to invite them to share the intimacy of His heart. This intimacy is where Jesus shares His nakedness by revealing the deep mysteries of His heart. Here, He is truly *Rabkumra*, a humble rabbi who makes Himself vulnerable to us. Most Christians are like the people of Israel in Exodus 24 who refused to enter the cloud. Instead, they told Moses to go into the cloud and then emerge from the cloud and tell them what God had to say. God's heart is available to everyone, but it is by invitation only, only to those who truly seek His heart on a daily basis, who search for Him with all their heart, soul, and might. (See Deuteronomy 4:29.) Many Christians would rather let the preacher do all the study and then share with them what he has learned in his Sunday morning sermon.

I was told in seminary that a pastor should spend up to forty hours a week studying the Word of God to prepare his twenty to forty-minute sermon. To try and share one minute for every hour one studies the Word of God, well, let me just say that there are a lot of good words that will never be preached.

"And ye shall seek me, and find me, when ye shall search for me with all your heart" (Jeremiah 29:13). That offer is to every believer, not just to the Bible college and seminary trained individual.

4

PROPHETS

"But when he saw many of the Pharisees and Sadducees
come to his baptism, he said unto them,
O generation of vipers."
—Matthew 3:7

Many Christians believe that there are prophets today, just as there were in the Old Testament. Many others believe the office of the prophet ended with the canonization of Scripture and that John the Baptist was the last prophet. Jewish rabbis tell me that with the death of the latter prophets, such as Haggai, Zechariah, and Malachi, at the very beginning of the second temple era, "the spirit of prophecy departed." This is found in the Talmud in Yoma 9b, Sanhedrin 11a, and Sotah 48b. Note that the Talmud said the spirit of prophecy *departed*; it did not cease, and many Jewish leaders point out that there have been a number of exceptional individuals throughout the Middle Ages and even modern times who have shown prophetic gifts. Since many Christians believe John the Baptist was the last prophet, we will use him to examine the office of the prophet.

Poor John is so misunderstood. He is often portrayed as a wild, maniacal doomsday prophet dressed in ill-fitted clothes, subsisting on insects and wild honey. He comes into town looking like a wild man, sending local residents running in terror and mothers hiding their children.

Let me give you a different picture of this man John the Baptist. Let's start with his clothing. It was not the clothing of a carelessly dressed crazy man. His clothing was carefully chosen to convey a message. His clothing was made of camel's hair, which was the skin of the animal without the coarse, itchy, stingy, thorny hair of the camel removed. He wore a garment that no normal person would wear because it was visibly uncomfortable. He was showing his rebellion against the corrupt governmental and religious leaders who made their fortunes off the backs of the common people, causing them to live in poverty and suffering as if they were living in clothing covered with camel's hair. He ate locust and honey not because he was living on the edge of insanity but because it was kosher (see Leviticus 11:21–23) and to show he followed religious law. Most likely, the locusts were a reference to a small bird that lived in the desert and would flock together in such swarms that Bedouins call them locusts and used them as a food source because they are easily caught; it is quite possible that this is what John ate.

John the Baptist would enter a town not as a madman but as a champion of the people. As people would gather around to hear the revolutionary message of this radical out to free them from the tyranny of those oppressing them, they would see that leather girdle or belt. Suddenly, their hero takes on a whole new meaning, for that leather belt is a symbol not seen for many, many years in the land of Israel. Mothers would tell their children of the days long past when men entered towns wearing leather belts, men who spoke from the heart of God, who prophesied of a coming day

Prophets 41

when justice would be meted out and the faithful to God would enter a new golden age. That leather belt was the symbol of a true prophet of God.

John's message was a simple one. In Aramaic, it is the word *tuwu*, which simply means to turn or return. In other words, if you have left your first love, your love for God, then return to it. If you have never loved God, then turn to Him and learn of His love. If you were baptized by John, it was simply a declaration that you were committing your life to love YHWH Elohim, the Lord God, with all your heart, soul, and might.

When John was baptizing, there were some Pharisees and Sadducees who attended the event. (See Matthew 3:7–10.) Pharisees were members of a religious order similar to religious orders of the Catholic church like Jesuits and Franciscans. Some are priests, and some are laymen, but all have committed their lives in a particular service to God.

Many Pharisees and Sadducees stood around and listened to John. Not all were bad as we get the impression from numerous sermons and Sunday school teachings. They firmly believed they were helping mankind and they were doing a lot of good. However, there was a corrupt element, causing many to give a sweeping consensus that all were bad.

It was these corrupt Pharisees and Sadducees that John called a generation or children of vipers. (See Matthew 3:7.) The word "viper" in the Aramaic is *akidneh*, which is a reference to a scorpion. When a male scorpion mates, it quickly dies, and when the young scorpion is born, it tears the body of the mother so that the mother dies. As a result, a baby scorpion is born into this world as an orphan without the guidance of a set of parents. John was simply declaring that the Pharisees and Sadducees were orphans. "Your parent Abraham died giving you birth, and you have long lost his guidance. However, your real parent is YHWH Elohim, the Lord God. Your salvation is not based upon your relationship with Abraham but with YHWH Elohim, the Lord God. *Tuwu.* Turn or return to your loving parent, YHWH Elohim, and you will no longer be orphans without any guidance."

We learn in Matthew 3:1 that *"in those days came John the Baptist, preaching in the wilderness of Judaea."* I don't know about you, but when I see the word "wilderness," I think of desert and uninhabitable land—except for the few creatures that wander through the desert. So, for whatever reason, I am picturing John the Baptist preaching to wild animals and bushes. The word "wilderness" is *eremo* in Greek, which means a place where there is no man. It conveys the idea of being uninhabited and desolate. It is a wasteland that is abandoned and/or a desert. Yet the verse says he was preaching. Preaching to whom? In Greek, the word for "preaching" is *kerysson*, which means to proclaim, to speak publicly with conviction and authority. In Aramaic the word for "preaching" is *makaraz* from the root word *karaz*, which means to preach or to announce or proclaim. However, it comes from a Semitic root found in both Akkadian and Sumerian languages that is used for a measuring container. When a preacher preaches, he is filling the congregation with the Word of God and then measuring that congregation according to the Word of God that filled them. Is the preacher giving too much or too little? Has the preacher carefully measured the Word of God that he is filling his congregation with? Sometimes, a preacher can fill his congregation with too much, causing them to overreact, or too little, causing them to give little response. I believe John the Baptist was not so much preaching as we understand preaching, but he was carefully measuring the Word of God that the Holy Spirit was filling him with. So, did John the Baptist do any real preaching in the wilderness? The word for "wilderness" in Aramaic is *bachuraba* from the root word *charav*, which is the word for a ploughed field. A field that will yield a harvest.

Prophets 43

The Talmud has numerous references to the wilderness or ploughed fields of Judaea. In Baba Kama 79b, Jews were encouraged to bring their cattle up to the wilderness or ploughed fields of Judaea. In fact, the *Shir Hashirim Rabbah* (Song of Songs midrash or commentary) indicates that there were at least five cities in the wilderness of Judaea that John the Baptist might have been preaching at, but I believe the word for preaching, *karaz* would indicate something more. This is likely a metaphor that he was preaching in a land ripe for harvest. He could have come into Jerusalem with a reputation as a mighty prophet of God from his preaching in the cities of the wilderness of Judaea, but the Rabbah goes on to say that this is the wilderness where the law was revealed, the tabernacle was built, the priesthood lived, the office of the Levites was established, and all good gifts that God gave to Israel were from the wilderness or ploughed fields of Judaea.

I believe this was more of a training ground for John the Baptist. It wasn't so much the miraculous work that preceded John the Baptist that gave him credibility when he came to Jerusalem; it was the fact that he spent time in this wilderness where all good gifts from God were believed to have come from. Maybe he wasn't so much preaching in the wilderness but was *karaz* in its true sense, being filled—that is, being filled with the Holy Spirit in the wilderness—and any proclamations or preaching he did was worshipping and praising God as he was learning to live a life in the Holy Spirit. If that is the case, poor John the Baptist spent thirty years preparing for just a few months of preaching before he was martyred.

Maybe there is a lesson in that for us. For many of us, we may spend a lifetime preparing for a ministry that could only last a few months. Yet, those few months could yield far more results than a few months of preparation and a lifetime of ministry. Astronauts spend practically their whole lives preparing for just a few days in outer space. An Olympic athlete will spend years training, sacrificing, and living in constant stress, pushing their body to its limit for just a few minutes in an athletic event. Soldiers will spend hours, months, and years just to prepare for a few minutes of combat. It is not unusual to spend far more time preparing for an event than the time spent performing for that event.

Rabbinical teaching on the life of the prophets has helped me realize that God could call you to spend years in preparation through Bible study, prayer, fasting, and maturing for just a short ministry that will bring about eternal results.

5

SCRIBES

"Woe unto you, lawyers! for ye have taken away the key of knowledge: ye entered not in yourselves and them that were entering in ye hindered."
—Luke 11:52

"I'm just a scholar made for you to teach."
—Claude Hopkins

Some translations say: "Woe to you experts in law," others say "law scholars" or "teachers in law." The word in Greek is *nomikois*, which means an expert in the law. In Aramaic, the word is *saphra*, where we get the word scribe. The scribes were the lawyers of their day. The Pharisees learned from the scribes, because they knew how to read and write, and not all Pharisees could. Thus, the interpretation of Scripture came mainly from the scribes who knew their advantage. They knew how to read where others didn't. If you did not know how to read, you would never dare to contradict

46 *What the Rabbis Know That I Never Learned in Church*

a scribe's interpretation because there would be no way for you to disprove it.

However, the Greek *nomikois* and Aramaic *saphra* not only refer to a scribe but to anyone who was literate and able to read and write. Thus, someone like Paul, who was not really a scribe but knew how to read and write, would be considered a *saphra*—and we all know how messed up his theology was until Jesus shined a light on him.

The lesson here is that just because someone portrays himself as a Bible scholar, it does not mean he is accurate in his interpretation. I confess I have pulled my PhD card several times to win an argument. If the person or people in the discussion group did not have a PhD, of if they hadn't spent forty years studying biblical languages every day for a minimum of three to four hours, they will usually acquiesce to my argument. I am telling you my dirty little secret because I am not the only one doing this. In fact, just let Toto pull back that curtain for a moment, and you will see that this great Hebrew Wizard is really just a friendly old man holding his kingdom together with a lot of bluff and bluster. Just like the scribe has the advantage over others because he was literate, I have an advantage because I'm literate in the biblical languages. Only someone else who has studied biblical languages would dare call me out, and if they do, we would end up fighting to see who has the better grasp of the language.

Once someone tells me of personal insight, if I say, "Well, that is not quite right because in the Hebrew…," did I just remove what Jesus calls the key of knowledge for this person? The word "key" here in Aramaic is *qalida*, which means to lock up, to make something disappear. Jesus said that these *saphras* had the ability to make knowledge disappear by simply saying: "I can read Scripture, and you can't." Yet God has a way of revealing Himself to people, and the Holy Spirit will guide them to the truth despite their so-called lack of biblical skills. But a pastor, teacher, Christian leader, or even a Chaim Bentorah who has studied in a Bible college and Seminary intimidates someone who has no background other than being self-taught. This causes them to bow to this *saphra*, causing them to assume the knowledge they received from the Holy Spirit is wrong.

This is what Jesus is condemning. God can reveal His Scriptures and knowledge without the help of people with their fancy degrees and titles. I conduct a Bible study on Saturday mornings, and as far as I know, none of the participants have a Bible school background. Yet, I am amazed at the wisdom that is shared. I even share their ideas with others.

Jesus further tells the scribes that *"ye have taken away the key of knowledge: ye entered not in yourselves,"* (Luke 11:52). Meaning you withhold knowledge that you have not even entered into yourselves. That implies talking about something you know nothing about. Alexander Pope said, "A little learning is a dangerous thing."[1] I have heard Christians who claim to have studied Hebrew say that the word "Elohim" is plural ... and thus in Genesis 1:1 where God is plural, it is addressing the Godhead, the Trinity. Such a statement shows their knowledge of grammatical rules is sorely lacking. Worse, by using their "look how smart I am" card, they will hinder someone who has no knowledge of biblical languages from entering into a personal revelation that God wants to reveal to them. They have to fact-check God with a human snake oil salesman.

Jesus said one final thing, *"...and them that were entering in ye hindered."* What Jesus was telling the *saphars*, He is also telling you and me: If you have an academic background or certain credentials, you can prevent people from entering knowledge that you have not even searched out yourself just by flashing a certificate saying you finished a Hebrew course. Jesus is reminding all

---

1. Alexander Pope, *An Essay on Criticism* (1709).

of us that all true knowledge comes from God, not from Chaim Bentorah or you.

I was really impressed by what one rabbi shared about his experience in the *Yeshivah*, which is a school focused on the study of rabbinic literature. Aside from lectures and classes, he and a study partner used the chavrusa style of learning. He and his study partner would examine the Torah in a classroom where the rabbi would sit at a desk. If he and his study partner struggled with the interpretation of a particular passage in the Torah, after a while, the rabbi would sit down at the desk with them and ask: "Well, what can you teach me?" The rabbi was highly respected with numerous academic achievements, yet he still felt he had more to he could learn from his students. That story made me think of what Jesus said in Luke 11:52 and the need for a teacher, scholar, or scribe to be humble and open to continued learning and not use his academic degree to intimidate others to follow his own agenda or belief system.

6

SADDUCEES, PHARISEES, AND SALVATION

"That if thou shalt confess with thy mouth the Lord Jesus, and shalt believe in thine heart that God hath raised him from the dead, thou shalt be saved. For with the heart man believeth unto righteousness; and with the mouth confession is made unto salvation."
—Romans 10:9–10

This is a pretty simple formula to get saved. Say the words "Lord Jesus" and believe He rose from the dead, and you've got it. It reminds me of a scene in the old movie *Ghostbusters* where they were hiring a new member of the team. The secretary ran off a list of "Do you believe in…" listing numerous supernatural events. The interviewee replied: "If there is a paycheck in it, I believe it."

I remember attending a church where the pastor made every new convert stand in front of the congregation and repeat the words: "Jesus Christ is Lord." After all, that is what Scripture says: you must confess with your mouth that Jesus Christ is Lord in order to be saved. I did not hear the pastor explain what it meant that Jesus Christ is Lord, nor did he explain what the words "Jesus," "Christ," and "Lord" really meant. It apparently was just good enough to recite those words like some incantation.

I recall another movie, which was a satire, in which the main character was in a monastery seeking a higher spiritual level. He was a complete annoyance to all the other monks, and when the chance to move him out came, the spiritual leader of the monastery gave him what he hoped would be good news: he could leave the monastery and live a regular life. Our hero protested that he was not ready to leave the monastery as he had not yet achieved enlightenment. The spiritual leader made a little gesture with his hand and said, "You've got it." Our hero again protested that he needed some token, and the spiritual leader quickly took a necklace around his neck and said: "Here, you can have mine." Our hero was now satisfied that he had obtained his enlightenment, and the monastery was now relieved of their annoyance.

All this is quite humorous, but I fear we have taken the very salvation, born-again experience of Jesus Christ to such a level. Say a sinner's prayer, utter a few words, and you've got heaven and all the perks that go with it. In my college years, I participated in many evangelistic programs. After all, one requirement of being a good Christian was that you were soul-winning. You would go up to some stranger and share a few Scripture verses, point out their need and how Jesus would meet that need, and then seal the deal with a sinner's prayer. At one point in my life, I got roped into selling insurance, although I never made it past the sale classes. But I remember the formula for making a cold call sale because it was identical to my evangelism classes.

I am convinced some people prayed the prayer just to get rid of me or else they felt sorry for me and didn't want to disappoint me.

Sadducees, Pharisees, and Salvation 51

In my heart, I feel I made very few converts. I soon began studying Aramaic and discovered the Aramaic word for "convert" was really a word for *submission*. We are not called to make converts; we are called to encourage people to submit to God. A convert means you get someone to accept your way of thinking, your theology, and your doctrine and make them a member of your sect. In encouraging someone to submit to God, you are putting the whole burden of doctrine, theology, and creeds into the hands of the Holy Spirit and not your denominational pastors and teachers. However, for some reason, we just can't seem to trust the Holy Spirit to get the new believer into the right doctrine and theology; we have to help the Holy Spirit out with His job. I've led a number of Catholics to the Lord who are still Catholic. However, their mass carries much more meaning for them and expresses their love for God.

Is saying, "Jesus Christ is Lord," and believing He rose from the dead all there is to salvation? That seems to be the formula that Paul gives. (See Romans 10:9.) But then he later talks about repentance, submission, grace, and faith. That is a lot more than reciting some words and believing in the resurrection.

We must first understand who Paul is speaking to. His audience on this occasion consisted of Sadducees. Many Christians do not know the difference between the Sadducees and the Pharisees. They were the two ruling groups among Jews in the first century.

The Pharisees strictly interpreted the Torah and developed an oral law to explain and expand on the Torah. They believed in Israel first and totally rejected any attempts of control by foreign powers like Rome.

The Sadducees believed the Torah had many different interpretations to fit the times. They also believed in a powerful controlling government like Rome, and that one should be more submissive to a global community.

Both Sadducees and Pharisees were members of the Sanhedrin, the highest court within the Jewish faith. The Pharisees and Sadducees were in constant conflict in doctrines and teachings. However, both groups were aligned in their dislike of Jesus and Paul, and considered them bad news, not good news.

The Sadducees and Pharisees held differing beliefs on the resurrection and the afterlife. The Sadducees did not believe in a resurrection or an afterlife; when you died, all existence ceased. The Pharisees had a concept of heaven and hell and believed that there would be a resurrection.

Thus, to suggest that Jesus Christ was Lord and to tell a Sadducee that they had to openly admit that Jesus was resurrected would be to deny their entire belief system. The Sadducees believed in a Messiah (Christ), but it could not be Jesus because they believed He was dead; He no longer existed. The Messiah had to be a living person who would lead them into a golden age. The only way to believe Jesus was the Messiah would be to admit what they did not believe: that He was resurrected.

The Sadducees were quite active in Judea, particularly Jerusalem, the home of the temple. The temple was their center of power, where the elite's authority, teachings, and doctrines were found. The priests and high priest dictated what people were to believe and how to interpret the Torah. The Pharisees controlled the synagogues where the power to determine doctrine and theology would be with the average shepherd.

The teachings of Jesus and Paul were found to be totally unsatisfactory to both parties. Their message consisted of the hope of an afterlife, and took away the requirement of following the Torah to be saved. People only needed faith in the Messiah called Jesus and the Torah was a good schoolteacher.

It would have been too much for a Sadducee to admit Jesus was not only the Messiah (Christ) but Lord as well. The word "Lord" in Greek is *kyrion*, which means the supreme authority and the master. In Aramaic, the word is *mara'*, which means a sovereign or an owner. The literal meaning is saying that Jesus is God Himself; a pretty heady admission for a Sadducee. The word "confess" in Aramaic is *yada'*, which is a cognate (a word that comes from the same root) to the same word in Hebrew for knowing or an intimacy. That is why Paul adds the words "with your mouth." The word "mouth" in Aramaic is *pum*, which is an expression of your thoughts; it doesn't necessarily mean your physical mouth. Besides words come from your vocal cords and out of your mouth. Your mouth is merely an opening, which is really the root idea of a *pum*, the edge or border of an opening.

I had the opportunity to drive a deaf and non-speaking man in my bus for disabled people. He was born this way so he cannot speak at all. He can offer grunts, groans, and a little whistle as nonverbal vocalizations. It is impossible for him to confess Jesus as Lord with words. So, is he out of luck in the salvation department? Hardly. We drove by a church, and he excitedly pointed to it and to himself. I am not sure if he attended the church as so much of church is verbal and auditory. He can't hear the sermon or music, but he can read sign language so perhaps they have someone in the church who uses sign language. Needless to say, he expressed his loyalty to God through *pum*. He publicly acknowledged Jesus as his Lord (at least, that is the way I took it), though not really with his mouth, but it still fits the word *pum*.

But let's analyze Romans 10:9–10 in light of a Sadducee. To acknowledge Jesus as the Messiah would be a sign of repentance, that he is turning away or rejecting the teaching of his worldview for what he believed the Holy Spirit was revealing to his heart. To acknowledge Him as Lord would be his declaration, whether verbal or in his actions, that this Jesus who was dead was his master, his ultimate authority. There would be a price to be paid for such an acknowledgment. He would be barred from the temple and from any association with his friends and even family who were members of the Sadducean sect. He would likely lose any job or means of financial support that he depended upon. It would be a complete surrender to God as God revealed Himself through the Holy Spirit in his life.

Such a move would involve not only an inner conviction but a personal experience in a relationship with God. Then he must believe in his heart that God raised Jesus from the dead. This was the ultimate rejection of the most fundamental belief of a Sadducee, that there was not only life after death but a resurrection into that life. But what that would include is an acknowledgment that there was an ultimate penalty for his sin after life and he would have to seek the final word in Paul's statement, salvation. Salvation from what? A good Jew would not have to be told what—it was obvious, sin. To ask for salvation would be to ask for forgiveness of sin.

Therein lies the whole plan of salvation. To recognize that there is an eternal penalty for sin, that we need a Messiah to redeem our sins, and we must believe that God sent an incarnation of Himself in the form of a human being who died and was resurrected. We need to repent of our sins and surrender ourselves, our lives, our livelihood—everything to God.

This all must be an expression of our heart. It should not be mere meaningless words or simply be a transmission from a human mouth. Instead, everything must come from the heart, the core of your passions, beliefs, and total self.

All this and you will have salvation. The Aramaic word used for "salvation" is *chia*, which means life or to live. In fact, in Aramaic it has the idea of a circle of life, or eternal life, a life that does not end. That would completely blow away a Sadducee who believed life ends in death. Paul was teaching that death is only the beginning of life.

7

THE GENTLE ONE—NICODEMUS

"There was a man of the Pharisees, named Nicodemus, a ruler of the Jews."
—John 3:1

We know little about Nicodemus other than what we find in John 3. We know he was a Pharisee. The word "Pharisee" in Aramaic is *perisha'*, which means to be set apart or separated. Basically, as explained in the last chapter, they were separated from the Sadducees, who favored Hellenization or assimilation into the Greek culture, which was the ruling force of that day. The Pharisees refused to be assimilated into the Greek culture, clinging to their Judaic roots. The Sadducees were formed from the elite and priestly tribe, whereas the Pharisees were descended from sages and rabbis and were more representative of the common people.

The Pharisaic beliefs evolved into the foundational, liturgical, and ritualistic beliefs of the rabbinic Judaism we have today. Rabbis have their roots in the Pharisaical sect. The Pharisees believed the Torah and the rest of what we have as the Old Testament today, which was canonized through the Sanhedrin to be the inspired Word of God. But they also believed that the oral laws or teachings (today known as the Talmud) were just as authoritative and inspired as the Torah.

The Sadducees, however, rejected everything except the original Torah or the Bible's first five books. This then created real doctrinal tension between the elite Sadducees and the Pharisees. The Sadducees and Pharisees each formed a distinct religious sect. A sect is a religious group that is the subset of a religion—in this case, Judaism—that shares the same foundational beliefs of that religion but will have marked differences concerning other doctrine. It is an offshoot of a larger group. For instance, in the mid-twentieth century, Christianity had a charismatic group that practiced more heartfelt worship and relationship with God than most mainline Protestant denominations. Charismatics believe in manifestations of the Holy Spirit through miraculous healings, speaking in tongues, and a personal love relationship with God. Evangelicals attended church and worshipped with a more traditional congregation who felt our role as Christians was to make the world a better place but rejected manifestations of the Holy Spirit that the Charismatics clung to. We could make a very loose comparison of the liberal element of the church were the Sadducees and the Charismatics with the Pharisees. From this picture, you can understand the conflict between the two groups.

The Jewish people of the first century generally sided with the Pharisees as they reflected a more traditional approach to their faith. Around 6,000 men officially declared themselves to be Pharisees and openly displayed their adherence to this sect. The majority of the Jewish population, if asked to choose which group they favored, would favor the less elite Pharisees. For the most part, the Pharisees were good, godly men seeking to serve God in the way their conscience dictated. What gave them such a bad name is that many looked down their noses upon those who were not as devoted. Their objection to Jesus might have been as much out of jealousy than anything else, as He was more highly regarded than they were as holy people. Their chief objection to Jesus was His flagrant disregard for oral law. As oral law was considered just as inspired as the Torah then, when Jesus healed on the Sabbath, which was not forbidden in the Torah but was forbidden in oral law, He was called a lawbreaker and sinner.

Pharisees have gotten a bad rap. In fact, today, if we wanted to speak badly about a religious person, we would call them a Pharisee. By that, we call them a hypocrite and infer they are a person who is really full of themselves, a real showboater. Although this is true of some Pharisees, not all were like that. Just as all pastors are not showboaters, arrogant, or take themselves too seriously. Most pastors are genuinely compassionate and caring. Nicodemus was one such Pharisee: he was one of the good Pharisees.

The name *Nicodemus* is hard to decipher. It appears to come from an Aramaic (Babylonian Aramaic) root for one who is gentle and kind. However, certain works by Josephus suggest it is a nickname of Greek origin, meaning conqueror of the people. In the Talmud Ta'anit 21a, it is suggested that his real name was the Hebrew name *Buni,* the discerning or understanding one. He was considered a leader among the Jews because he was a member of the Sanhedrin. He came to Jesus by night, not because he was ashamed or fearful of the talk among the people that he was associating with Jesus. In fact, it would have been quite the opposite that a great leader would seek to dialogue with an itinerate teacher. Approaching Jesus at night was more of an indication of a less formal dialogue. As there were no electric lights, people often went to bed as soon as the sun went down. They would sleep for a few hours and then get up for a couple of hours to socialize, and then go back to bed until sunrise. This is a practice that still

58   *What the Rabbis Know That I Never Learned in Church*

continues in parts of the world that have no electricity or artificial lighting. Hence for Nicodemus to meet with Jesus at night was not a secret meeting but an informal meeting.

The only mention of Nicodemus is in the book of John, where he appears in three places. First, in John 3, where he meets Jesus at night. The second is in John 7:50, where he is in dialogue with his colleagues in the Sanhedrin and again in John 19 after the crucifixion of Jesus. The only extra biblical appearance of Nicodemus is in a book called the gospel of Nicodemus. This book is a fourth-century medieval work, and despite its claim to have been written by Nicodemus, there is no evidence of this; in fact, the writing style indicates various authors and points to pagan origins. It is generally rejected by scholars as authentic.

There is a reference, previously mentioned, in the Jewish Talmud to one who might be Nicodemus. The reference is to Nicodemus Ben Gurion in Ta'anit 19b and Gittin 56a and he is also present in the works of Josephus in the *Jewish Wars*. He is described as a wealthy but generous Jewish man who lived in the first century in Jerusalem and who suffered the loss of his wealth in retaliation by the Zealots when he tried to broker a peace with the Roman Emperor Vespasian through the emperor's son Titus. He was also considered a miracle worker. This would have made Nicodemus a young man about the same age as Jesus or younger when he met with Him.

If Nicodemus Ben Gurion is the same man as the Nicodemus of John 3, then the fact that he was a man who worked miracles would explain the purpose of his visit with Jesus. Nicodemus made no reference to the teachings of Jesus, only to the fact that he performed miracles. As a holy man himself, Nicodemus would have desired to know the secret of Jesus's ability to perform miracles. This explains the abrupt reference by Jesus to being born again to enter the kingdom of God. In Jewish thought of that day, the kingdom of God was knowledge of God and how He worked.

In the Aramaic, Nicodemus's response to Jesus saying you had to be born again was more a statement than a question. (See John 3:4.) In other words, he asked: "So you are not referring to entering your mother's womb and being born again?" Jesus's response to that was that one must be born of water and the Spirit (verse 5). He was not referencing baptism. Baptism of that day was a way of identifying with a certain teacher. Followers were baptized in the name of that teacher. This is why Jesus had to be baptized by John the Baptist, because He needed to identify with a certain teaching. John the Baptist was a forerunner for Jesus in the sense of laying the groundwork for the message of Jesus. When He was baptized with John's baptism, people knew where Jesus stood doctrinally.

Nicodemus would have recognized the water Jesus was talking about as living water, which was Jesus's message to the woman at the well in the next chapter. (See John 4:6–30.) Living water was a first-century Jewish symbol of purification. One must be born purified. In Aramaic, there is the preposition *Mem* in front of the word water, so it is being born from water—that is, born from the cleansing of sins and from the Spirit of God.

Jesus, using the techniques familiar to rabbis of His time, made an illustration of our relationship with God through a marriage analogy. Before a Jewish wedding, the bride and groom must take a bath in a mikvah as a purification ceremony. Then they stand under a canopy where they exchange their vows. After they say their vows, they step through the canopy like walking through a door and step into a new life joined in the spirit as one. They are declared to be born again, that is, entering a new life. A life that does not center around oneself, but now centers around two people. The couple does not share fifty-fifty in resources but one hundred percent to one hundred percent. They make no decisions or major purchases without consulting each other,. The two work as one. This is what it means to be born again in God. We are literally married to God so that one hundred percent of His is one hundred percent of ours. We do not give Him ten percent of our earnings and keep ninety percent for ourselves. One hundred percent is God's as well as ours. We become one with God in Spirit. We make no decisions without consulting God; whatever we do, we do as unto God.

When Nicodemus asked Jesus how this could be, Jesus said: *"Art thou a master of Israel, and knowest not these things?"* (John 3:10). Many preachers today teach salvation by grace and faith, not by works. Yet, in the same breath, they insist that you must attend church every Sunday and give ten percent of your income as a tithe. But ask that preacher if they can still be saved even if they don't go to church or pay a tithe; you may get a lot of hemming and hawing. *"We speak that we do know, and testify that we have seen; and ye receive not our witness"* (verse 11). In other words, Jesus was telling Nicodemus very politely, "If you have to ask Me what it means, then you do not practice what you preach."

8

BIND AND LOOSEN

"And the key to the house of David will I lay upon his shoulder; so he shall open, and none shall shut; and he shall shut, and none shall open."
—Isaiah 22:22

"And I will give unto thee the keys of the kingdom of heaven: and whatsoever thou shalt bind on earth shall be bound in heaven: and whatsoever thou shalt loose on earth shall be loosed in heaven."
—Matthew 16:19

Matthew 16:19 has become a popular verse in recent years for teaching about the power of prayer. If two or three are gathered together then whatever you bind on earth will be bound in heaven and hence God will grant our prayer request. (See Matthew 18:19 and 16:19.) Yet this phrase *"whatever you bind on earth will be bound in heaven and whatever you loose on earth shall be loosed in heaven,"* is really a common rabbinical phrase that was used by religious leaders during the time of Jesus. To understand this passage from a rabbinical standpoint, we need to go to the Old Testament and the book of Isaiah.

In Christianity, we generally accept that Isaiah 22:22 is Messianic. I am aware and agree one hundred percent. I am not a Catholic, but I do take a very Catholic interpretation of Matthew 16:19. That does not mean that I believe the authority given to Peter by Jesus was intended to have apostolic succession. I find no scriptural basis to believe that such powerful authority was granted to Peter to pass down. I hold that it was not meant to live beyond Peter's lifetime. Jesus gave this authority to help in the establishment of the church.

With regard to Isaiah 22:22, the historical background takes us to Eliakim, who was the prime minister or finance minister to King Hezekiah. God used him as a picture of the Messiah, and I believe Jesus, as a good religious teacher, used this biblical picture to explain the authority he would grant to Peter. This leads to the obvious conclusion that I reject the popular interpretation of Matthew 16:19 that Jesus is granting us the authority to rule over demonic spirits. Although I believe we have that authority through the blood of Jesus Christ and the power of the Holy Spirit, I do not believe it was granted here, nor do I accept the many other interpretations that seem to be coming down the pike on Matthew 16:19. As there are many interpretations of this verse, allow me to share an interpretation from something I learned from rabbis, which I personally find to be a more accurate interpretation. Yes, I am waving my flag of solidarity with Jewish teaching here. But before you pick up rocks to stone me, let me just explain why I believe what I do, and why I am walking through this mine field. My study partner and I have been discussing this matter of religious bondage and this is how I address this problem.

Bind and Loosen 63

In Matthew 16:19, Jesus gave the keys to the kingdom to Peter and told him that whatever he binds on earth will be bound in heaven, and whatever he looses on earth will be loosed in heaven. The word "binding" in Greek is *dein* and "loose" is *luein*. The Septuagint uses these very same words for the Hebrew words *asar* and *hitir*. In my Aramaic Bible, the Peshitta shows the Aramaic word *'esar* for bind, which is cognate to the Hebrew word *'asar*, and the Aramaic word *shira* for "loose," which is also cognate to the Hebrew word *hitir*. Both words are legal terms found throughout the Mishnah and Talmud and represents forbidding and permitting. The council of sages and rabbis of the Sanhedrin were granted the authority (by man) to *asar or 'esar* (bind) and *hitir or shira* (loose or set free from) Jews to aspects of the law. It was believed that whatever the rabbis bound (*'asar, 'esar*) on earth was bound in heaven and whatever they loosed (*hitir, shira*) on earth was loosed in heaven. This was recorded in the tradition of the fathers during the time of Jesus, which eventually became the Talmud. The word "heaven" was just another term used to represent God so one would not speak the sacred name of God. Thus, it was believed that what the Sanhedrin ruled whether to *bind* (*'asar, 'esar*) or *loose* (*hitir, shira*) was automatically ratified by God. It would seem that Jesus used this same popular expression to grant similar authority to Peter to resolve future disputes in the establishment of the church.

We find one such example of this binding (*'asar, 'esar*) and loosing (*hitir, shira*) to take place in Acts 15, where the apostles and elders convened in a sort of Church Sanhedrin in Jerusalem to address the issue as to whether Gentiles were bound to the law. In Acts 15:10, we find Peter exercising this rabbinic authority granted to him by the very lips of Jesus of binding (*'asar, 'esar*) and loosing (*hitir, shira*) to declare that the commandments were too heavy for the Gentiles and that they should be loosed from the obligations of the law. In verse 20, James chimed in and said that he agreed but

64   *What the Rabbis Know That I Never Learned in Church*

that the Gentiles should still be bound by laws that the Jews considered universal prohibitions such as murder, adultery, idolatry, and so on. In verse 22 it appears everyone gave a hearty amen and then sent Paul and Barnabas out to spread the Word.

From this, I believe the issue of the law and our obligation to the law was resolved and later confirmed by the apostle Paul in the first century and under the authority of binding (*'asar, 'esar*) and loosing (*hitir, shira*) granted to Peter by Jesus. We, as Gentiles, are not bound to the Judaic laws that are indigenous to Judaism, such as the dietary laws, laws of festivals, tithing, and so on. But we are bound to those laws that are considered universal laws such as not committing murder, adultery, idolatry, and so forth. It helps to look through Jewish literature to find out what the universal laws are, but the Holy Spirit does a better job at that within our own hearts.

Did I say Gentiles were loosed from the law of tithing? I see many of you picking up those rocks again. But hear me out. Not even the Jews practice tithing because it is a law that applies only to the temple, and because the temple no longer exists, this law is no longer applicable to anyone. Even the apostle Paul addresses this, *"Every man according as he purposeth in his heart, so let him give; not grudgingly, or of necessity: for God loveth a cheerful giver"* (2 Corinthians 9:7). The word "cheerful" is *chadi* in Aramaic, which is a sense of pure joy. In this context Paul is saying we are to give simply for the joy of giving, no ulterior motives. We are not to give grudgingly or as expressed in the Aramaic word *kariutha*, which means pain or misfortune. That is, we are not to give if some misfortune or pain comes upon us, so we give, hoping that God will deliver us from our misfortune or relieve our suffering. We are not to give out of necessity, which in Aramaic is the word *qatiria* meaning conspiracy. That is a secret plot to obtain something illegally. In this context, Paul is addressing those who give thinking their gift will bribe God or manipulate God to giving them a blessing.

I do not oppose tithing. If we want to have a church building where we can meet together for the pure joy of Christian fellowship and worship and we wish to have someone lead that church, we should pay our fair share to establish such an institution. However, from a Jewish understanding of tithing, we are under no scriptural obligation or law to give ten percent of our income to the church. We do it out of the pure joy of having an opportunity and a place to worship in fellowship with other believers.

The point is, if we look at Isaiah 22:22 and Matthew 16:19 from a Jewish historical and cultural context, it would help us understand the significance of Acts 15 and maybe cause us to rethink our interpretation of Matthew 16:19. Also, it may help us gain some insight into our obligation of the law. Many rabbis have told me that as a Gentile, I am not *'asar, 'esar* (bound) to the 513 commandments and *hitil, shita* (loosed) from all but the Ten Commandments. Some have even said I am only bound to three of the ten commandments. But I prefer to take my cues direct from the Spirit of God.

9

THE SECOND IS LIKE THE FIRST

"And God said, Let us make man in our image,
after our likeness."
—Genesis 1:26

"And thou shalt love the Lord thy God with all thy heart,
and with all thy soul, and with all thy mind, and with all
thy strength: this is the first commandment. And the second
is like, namely this, Thou shalt love thy neighbour as thyself.
There is none other commandment greater than these."
—Mark 12:30–31

There is an old rabbinic trick that ancient Jewish teachers would use. The Jews recognized that certain laws were seemingly more important than others. For instance, one was to honor their parents, but they were also to honor a mother bird. Obviously, it is more important to honor your parents. However, what ancient teachers would refer to two laws by saying, "The second is like the first," indicating that the seemingly lesser law is just as important as a law that seems to have greater value.

I remember a time when I was experiencing a physical affliction and prayed for healing. I prayed in faith, believing, and as the preachers told me how to pray, but I was not healed. I begged and pleaded with God and still nothing. I finally shook my fist at heaven and cried out: "God, You are God, You are a spirit. You don't have a physical body, so how do You know what it is like to suffer physical pain? Huh? Huh? You have a lot of nerve to expect me to go through all this suffering when You sit up there in heaven, free from any suffering. Why don't You come down here on earth in a human body for a while and see what it is like, then maybe You would be more incline to listen to our pleas for healing."

That is when it struck me, He did just that. He did come to earth in a human body, and He did suffer torment and death. He does know, He does understand. Once more, we are made in His image, which is *tselem* in Hebrew, a word used for a shadow. We are only shadows of what He is. Image does not mean two arms, two legs, a face, and so forth. It means we have emotions and a heart like His. Just as we experience a broken heart, He too experiences a broken heart. "*The LORD is nigh unto them that are of a broken heart*" (Psalm 34:18). Why is He near to the brokenhearted? It is because we break His heart every day. He knows and understands a broken heart becuase who can empathize more than someone who has had their heart broken on a daily basis?

The words in Hebrew for a "broken heart" are *nisheberi lev*. *Nisheberi* comes from the root word *shabar*, which means to crush, shatter, demolish, or destroy. Does that sound like your heart? Well, it describes what we do to God's heart when we seek other gods of this world for comfort, strength, support, and security. Note that *nisheberi* is in a niphal form—it is reflexive; God is allowing Himself, voluntarily opening Himself up to a broken heart. He is God, He doesn't have to suffer a broken heart. Why does He put Himself through all that if He doesn't have to do it?

The answer to that lies in Genesis 1:26. Not only were we created in His image—that is, to have a mind and heart like His—but we were also created in His likeness. Now, in English, the words "image" and "likeness" appear to have the same or similar meanings. However, the Hebrew word for "likeness" is *dumah*, which is not an appearance but a quality; it is likeness in value. He created us human beings to be of equal value to Himself. This word goes even further. This is not just equal in value but equal to *or more* in value.

What does that mean to be in His likeness, His *dumah?* Check out your average parent. I listened to a documentary on Tom Brady, a famous former professional football star. He related how his parents sacrificed and gave so much to help him realize his dream of making it in professional football. He told how his father would spend hours with him when he was a child, throwing a ball to him because he knew his son had this dream, and this father sacrificed time he could have spent on other things just to help his son grow up to realize his dream. I mean, we expect this of a parent because a parent has that sacrificial love. To them, it is no sacrifice; they would do anything for their child's happiness and sometimes even lay down their lives for their child as that child was created in their *dumah*. They were created to be of equal or more value to them than they are to themselves.

I recently read about how a rather famous celebrity had died in an auto accident. The investigation into the accident revealed that, in a split second before the tragic event occurred, the celebrity instinctively threw his body over his wife to protect her from the impact. She survived; he didn't. The investigators said had he not thrown his body on top of her, he would have survived, but she would have been killed. This man loved his wife, *dumah*, of equal value and more than himself, more than his own life. He did not even have time to think about it and decided to sacrifice His life for his beloved. He loved his wife so much it was just instinctive that He would sacrifice his life for her. He didn't have time to contemplate whether he wanted to give up his life for her, he didn't have time to weigh the issue in his mind. His love was so deep for her that there was no need to make any decision. That decision was made when he fell in love with her.

That is *dumah*, to be in the likeness of someone or something. To value someone as much or more than yourself. That is how God created us, to be of equal value to Himself. Yes, He even values us more than Himself, more than His own existence.

Now consider this from the New Testament. In Mark 12, we have the story of a scribe who comes to Jesus and asks Him what the greatest commandment is. Jesus answers that it is to love the Lord your God with all your heart, soul, mind, and strength. Then he adds: *"And the second is like, namely this, Thou shalt love thy neighbour as thyself. There is none other commandment greater than these"* (Mark 12:31). In Aramaic it reads, "The second is like unto the first." As explained earlier, this is an old rabbinic expression and trick to place two things together as equal in value. Thus, it is just as important and of equal value to love your neighbor as yourself.

How does this relate to Genesis 1:26? It relates to *dumah*, equal value. God has placed us human beings to be of equal or greater value than Himself, but more than that, He is the poster child, the role model for *dumah*. He expects us not to do anything that He would not be willing to do Himself. Thus, if He values us of equal or more value than Himself, *dumah*, He expects us to at least love our neighbor as much as ourselves and, if possible, even more. To follow His example.

Just who is our neighbor? The word in Aramaic for "neighbor" is *barabibad*, which comes from the root word *bar*. This is also the word for a son but in this form, it means a foreigner. It is where we get our English word "barbarian." In a sense, we are all brothers

The Second Is Like the First 71

and sisters as we are descended from the same parents, Adam and Eve. Over a period of thousands of years our brothers and sisters started to establish their own generations and before long our relationship with each other becomes more and more distant. Yet in God's eyes and mind, like it or not, the most despicable world leader or criminal is just a distant relative of you and me. Not only are we related to them by our common ancestors Adam and Eve, but we can trace it back even further: we are related by a common creator, God. For most of us, we love our immediate family, our brothers, sisters, and parents, which we say are related to us by blood. But the simple fact is that we are all related by blood. In God's eyes, that world leader or criminal is just as much your brother-by-blood relationship as you are to that brother or sister you keep on your speed dial, that you would drop everything for to run to their aid.

In Luke 10:25–37 Jesus told the story about a Jewish man, or so it is implied, who is robbed by bandits stripping him of his clothing. Clothing was a very valuable in those days, as most people only had one set of garments. Thus, he was stripped naked, beaten, and left for dead alongside the road. First a Jewish priest, then a Levite, two men considered to be the holiest among the Jews, came by, but neither helped the man. Finally, a Samaritan happens upon the traveler.

It is interesting that Jesus selected a Samaritan because the Jews hated Samaritans and vice versa to such a degree that the Jews destroyed the Samaritans' temple on Mt. Gerizim. Tensions between them were particularly high in the early decades of the first century because Samaritans had desecrated the Jewish temple at Passover with human bones. Yet geographically, they were neighbors. Even the scribe apparently hesitated to answer Jesus's question directly when he asked, "*Now which of these three do you think seemed to be a neighbor to him who fell among the robbers?*" (Luke 10:36 WEB). It is suggested that the old scribe himself hated the Samaritans so much that he could not even answer directly—"The Samaritans." Instead, he could only say, *"The one who had mercy on him"* (Luke 10:37 NIV). Yet despite that hatred, it was the Samaritan who helped the badly beaten and robbed Jewish man.

Who is our neighbor? I had a woman on my disability bus who was injured in an auto accident while going out to get formula for her baby. A man driving at a high rate of speed under the influence of alcohol turned right into her vehicle, which was stopped at a red light. The collision totaled her car, while the other driver fled the scene. The police caught up to and arrested him, but shockingly, he was released from jail the following day. The case against him was also dismissed. He was an undocumented immigrant, yet to be deported, who was cited for driving without a license, without proof of insurance, and with a DUI. The woman suffered a permanent disabling injury leaving her with constant pain, which her doctor said she will live with the rest of her life. This situation became even more difficult as she and her husband were forced to move because the man from the accident would arrive outside their house and mock them. He scornfully used his undocumented status to mock his legal proceedings, laughed at her disability, and bragged that he was above prosecution. The woman's insurance did not cover the treatment for her disability or her medical bills. The accident and insurance situation left the woman and her family in deep medical debt. While her family replaced the car, she witnessed the man keying the new car and laughing in her face. She called the police but they were unable to help her and her family. The man continued to laugh, mock, and jeer the woman, her disability, and her family. He bragged how there were people who sympathized with him in fighting deportation and prosecution.

What would you do if you found the man from the accident lying on the street having a heart attack and calling out to you for help? Would you help him, knowing how evil he is and what he did to the woman and her family? Would you call an ambulance and pay for that ambulance? He is your *barabibad* (emphasis on the last three letters), your foreign neighbor. I am sure that that is how that scribe felt. Could you value that person as you value yourself?

How should we react when we see the DUI driver, or a dictator guilty of mass atrocities? It is easy to hate the sin, but can we really love the sinner? That is hard, very hard, and yet God values that DUI driver as much as Himself; He values the dictator as much as Himself.

Through my interactions with various Jewish people, I have noticed a prevalent sentiment among many Jews regarding the Holocaust during World War II. Over six million Jews were murdered, and I spoke with a few who had parents or grandparents and other relatives who perished in the death camps. They speak of the lessons they learned throughout their life to forgive and not carry bitterness. It is doubtful they learned to love the Nazis, but they had to learn to forgive and not harbor anger. I am not saying God caused the Holocaust or even allowed it, but He is an opportunist and the Jews as His chosen people are meant to be spiritual role model to the world. The attempts of these Jewish people to forgive and not harbor bitterness toward their enemies has had a profound effect on my attitude toward those who have done wrong to me.

10

WHERE TWO OR THREE ARE GATHERED

"Again I say unto you, That if two of you shall agree on earth as touching any thing that they shall ask, it shall be done for them of my Father which is in heaven.
For where two or three are gathered together in my name, there am I in the midst of them."
—Matthew 18:19–20

"Where two or three are gathered together to study Torah, the Divine Presence is in their midst."
—The Talmud

The most common interpretation of Matthew 18:19–20 is such a sacred cow for Western Christians that if anyone dare suggest that our interpretation is even slightly contrary to the standard interpretation, it would be like suggesting that apple pie and mothers were un-American. Yet, every time I attend a prayer meeting and I hear someone say, "Let's agree in prayer," I can't help but stop and think about what they are saying. Is God going to be more motivated to answer a prayer if three people are praying for a matter versus just one?

I remember a well-known Christian personality suffered an accident and people all over the world were praying for their recovery. If I had the same accident, I could count on one hand the number of people who would pray for good old Chaim's recovery. Who stands the better chance of getting healed, Chaim with his five people praying for him, or the one who has thousands praying for them? Does God have some accountant angel up there in heaven with a calculator, wearing a visor, frantically adding up the number of people praying? And when it hits certain number, a messenger runs to God saying, "Hey God, a million prayers for this old boy. He has won the spiritual lottery! Send forth the healing waves." What if I am alone and I have no one to pray in agreement with me over an urgent matter? Is God up there in heaven shaking His head saying, "Chaim, Chaim, when are you going to learn you need at least two or three others agreeing with you in prayer before you can expect an answer?" Doesn't that contradict what it tells us in James 5 that the prayer of a (that is one) righteous man can avail much? (See James 5:16.)

In Greek, Matthew 18:19 literally reads, "Again, amen, I am saying to you that if ever two shall be in agreement out of you on the land in every matter that they are requesting it shall be becoming to them." Here is the key: the idea is not to be ganging up on the Lord and storming the palace, hoping He will give in and give you what you want. It is the idea that someone is agreeing with you, that your request is within the will of God. If that person does not agree, then a third person is called in to arbitrate the dispute and bring everyone into agreement. In James 4:3 we learn that *"ye ask, and receive not, because ye ask amiss, that ye may consume it upon your lusts."* The word "amiss" in Aramaic is *dabishiait*, which has the idea of asking in the flesh. In other words, you are praying for fleshly desires and not heavenly desires.

The Aramaic word Jesus used for "agree" is *nashatuon,* which in this particular grammatical form means to be found worthy. People have various motives when they come together to pray. Some like to show off their piousness, some like to preach a little sermon, some like to show off their great oratory ability, and some just pray out of group pressure. If only two or three are praying the fervent prayer of a righteous person, and they are worthy—that is, they are not asking to fulfill their own fleshly desires or lust but only to fulfill the will of God—the request will be granted. Where two or three are found worthy means that they are not asking for their own vanity but for the sake of the kingdom of God.

Jesus almost quotes verse 20 directly from the oral tradition that was later recorded in the Talmud. The Talmud teaches, "Where two or three are gathered together to study Torah, the Divine Presence is in their midst." The Talmud admonishes one never to study the Torah alone. Ancient Jews, and even Jews today, would never study Scripture alone. Some people would even hire someone to study the Torah with them. Of course, you are going to say that the passage in Matthew is clearly speaking about our prayer requests and not studying the Bible. We would say that because our mindset in our Western culture is "me" oriented. To many people, God is merely a celestial vending machine. Pop in a few token prayers, push the button, and out comes what you want. For many in our Western society, Christianity is a marriage of convenience with God. The purpose of such a marriage is to ensure that one's personal needs come first. In Jewish thinking, however, it is a marriage of love where the needs of the other come first. So, we approach Matthew 18 not as "Ah ha, a formula to get my prayers answered" but rather as another deep teaching by Jesus. The reason the Talmud says, "Where two or three are gathered together..." and most likely why Jesus used this common expression of His day is that when two people study together, a problem sometimes arises. The two may disagree over how to interpret a passage. When this happens, a third person, often a rabbi, is brought in to bring the two into an agreement. It also happens when we make a request to God. We should have a prayer partner who will confirm our request. If there is a disagreement that the request is not of God but of the flesh, you may need to bring in a third party to help bring all into agreement that they are praying the will of God and not asking out of fleshly motives.

I have to admit I have found more comfort from this passage of Scripture when I view it from a Jewish standpoint of seeking the unity of the body rather than offering a formula to bribe God for an answer to your prayers.

11

THE DEVIL

"Submit yourselves therefore to God. Resist the devil,
and he will flee from you."
—James 4:7

There are few Christians who do not know this verse by memory. As to whether they know it by heart, that is debatable. Every modern English translation renders the concept in this verse as "resist." What does it mean to resist the devil? Merriam-Webster defines "resist" as: to exert force in opposition, to exert oneself to counteract or defeat, and to withstand the force or effect of.[2] If we submit ourselves to God, all we have to do is oppose the devil. Maybe there is more to this than we realize.

In Greek the word for "submit" is *hypotagete*, which is to rank or place oneself under a specific plan or arrangement. Thus, we can only resist the devil when we place ourselves in God's plan,

---

2. "Resist." Merriam-Webster.com Dictionary, Merriam-Webster, https://www. merriam-webster.com/dictionary/resist. Accessed 19 Nov. 2024.

the center of His will. The center of God's will is the safest place we can be. In Aramaic the word used for "submit" is 'evad. In this context, it has the idea of ownership and/or enslavement. We are to enslave ourselves to the will of God. When the enemy finds out who owns us, he will not hang around.

But I think there is another reason he will not want to be around us. When we resist him, what are we doing? In Greek, the word "resist" is *antistete*, which means to set against, to withstand, to take a complete stand against, or to refuse to be moved. That is reasonable, but I don't feel that is enough to get the enemy to move.

Take a look at the word for "devil." James uses the Aramaic word *satana*, which could be rendered as Satan, but it has an Aleph suffix indicating a definite article. It is cognate to the word *hasatan* in Hebrew as found in the book of Job. In Hebrew, the definite article is a *Hei* prefix and like in Aramaic this would not make the word a proper name, which is why translators render this as simply "the devil" in the book of James. Scripture does not even dignify the old buzzard with a name.

The word "devil" in Greek is *diabolo*. It means slanderous or accuser. That is exactly the meaning of the Aramaic word *satana*. So, what are we resisting? It is the enemy's accusations against us. It is his slander, accusing us of things we are and are not guilty of. He loves to slander us and fill us with false guilt.

Have you ever called upon God to help you, to protect you, to heal you, or any other request and then you hear a little voice in your head that says, "Who do you think you are? Do you honestly believe God will answer that prayer or even listen to you after what you did? Be reasonable, you don't deserve that answer to your prayer."

You know what we do: we don't resist that thought. Instead, we play right into his little game and agree with him. What we should do is point our finger at the devil and say, "You are right, I don't deserve it, but you are also a liar. Jesus shed His blood, died on a cross, and rose again. All those reasons why God should not answer my prayer no longer exist. They are washed away in the blood of the Lamb." If we do that in the center of God's will, the accuser will flee from us. The word "flee" in Greek is *pheuxetai*, which means to escape or shun. But that is not the whole story. Why does he try to escape or shun us?

In Aramaic the word used is *'eraq*, which means to be in pain and torment. He will flee from us in pain and torment. But why will he be in pain and torment from us simply *antistete*, standing up to him, resisting him?

The Aramaic word used by James is *qom*. It means to stand against something, like the Greek word *antistete*, but its Semitic root tells us much more. It is used for growing maize, also known as Indian corn. The people of Egypt and in the Mesopotamian area used to feed their livestock with it. Almost 50% of the crops in the Middle East during the first century were maize. The Middle Eastern climate and abundant sunlight allowed maize to flourish and resist pestilences prone to attack; it does not grow as strongly and may die in shaded areas.

You see, just resisting the accusations of the devil will not cause him to flee in pain and torment. We must be in the center of God's will, and we must stand in the light of God. The devil hates God's light, and he knows that the blood of Jesus is what gives us the benefit of that light. With sin in our lives, we cannot endure the light of God just like the enemy, and the enemy has us right where he wants us. But if we are cleansed, and washed clean of all our sins, the light of God will shine upon us, and it will cause the enemy pain and torment. The devil was once the light bearer and he lost that position. It now belongs to us; that is why he hates us. For now, he cannot even stand to be in the light of God, so he will flee in torment and pain when God casts His Light upon him through us, His Light bearers.

The Jewish concept of the *satana* is quite different than my view or that of Christianity. Within Judaism Satan is not a sentient being but a metaphor to describe the *yetzer hara*—that is, the evil inclination in each individual that tempts one to disobey God. *Yetzer hara* is found in Genesis 6:5: "*And God saw that the wickedness of man was great in the earth, and that every imagination of the thoughts of his heart was only evil continually.*" The word "imagination" in Hebrew is *yetzer* and *hara* is from the root word *ra'a'*, which is the word for evil with a definite article *Hei*. Literally, it is "the evil of the imagination." *Yetzer* is a word for behavioral inclination. Hence the *yetzer hara'* is your evil inclination and is, in a way, what we in Christianity would call our sinful nature. The only place in the Old Testament where *hasatan* is viewed as a sentient being is in the book of Job. Here *hasatan* is pictured as an adversary who questions the piety of Job. He confronts God and declares that Job only serves God because God pays him so well. Take it all away and he will curse God. In other words, humankind is basically a selfish race that will serve God only for the benefits and not out of true love. This whole heavenly scene with *hasatan* challenging God is viewed as a metaphor by Jewish scholars, and the idea of an actual creature with a kingdom of his own over some metaphysical realm is not really accepted by Judaism.

Yet, the role of the *hasatan* in the book of Job does sort of muddy up this view that Satan is not a sentient being. From this passage many Jewish scholars conclude that God created an angel to play the role of a tempter who intentionally encourages people to do something forbidden by God. They put him in the role of a messenger who is subservient to God and thus is not a fallen angel who is sent to hell where he begins to fight against God. He was created to be a presence on earth with a mission to provoke people to disobey God's will, and to give the human creature an opportunity to exercise a free will.

The Jews have a problem with a sentient being that is so powerful that it feels it can fight against God. Such a belief is not compatible with Jewish belief as there is no power of evil independent of God; otherwise, it would show a lack of God's all-inclusive control and power.

> *I form the light, and create darkness: I make peace, and create evil: I the* LORD *do all these things.* (Isaiah 45:7)

To many orthodox Jewish teachers, *hasatan* is a spiritual entity that is completely faithful to its maker God. The Zohar explains it with a parable about a king who hires a prostitute to seduce his son to test his son's morality and worthiness. The prostitute is devoted to the king and like the king wants the son to stand firm and reject her advances. Thus, *hasatan* is just another one of many spiritual messengers or angels that God sends to accomplish His purpose in the creation of man.

This teaching seems to be filled with many holes. Chief among them is why would God deliberately create a being to seduce a human creature away from Him? The answer is where I find something taught by the rabbis that truly enlightens my understanding of a relationship with God. Love finds its greatest fulfillment when it is given by choice.

Robotics and artificial intelligence are quickly reaching a point where an android—that is, a robot that appears identical to a human being and expresses emotions like a human being—can be manufactured. One of the greatest markets would be to make a female robot that would be manufactured to be a real-life companion that appears and acts like a real woman. The greatest problem would be that to give this robot free will would risk the owner being rejected by his android companion and hence reduce its marketing value. Yet, without free will to choose to love, the real emotional fulfillment of love could not happen. God has created a world filled with living creatures that have no free will. The animal kingdom is filled with many different species that do not have the ability to choose or reject God. Only the human being was created with this free will, with the ability to accept or reject God. Only human beings can give God what He truly desires, and that is someone who chooses to love Him or reject him.

As a pastor, I would officiate at wedding ceremonies, and I would always look forward to seeing the joy on the faces of the bride and groom when I announce them as husband and wife. For some reason, it is at this moment the couple is struck with the reality that of all the possible life partners among the billions of human beings on this earth that could have been chosen, this one individual chose them. At any time, they could have backed out of the ceremony but by an act of free will they did not because they truly loved this person that they would devote their lives to.

Let me explain this through the Jewish understanding of why God hardened Pharaoh's heart. Exodus 7:3 says, *"And I will harden Pharaoh's heart, and multiply my signs and my wonders in the land of Egypt."* I have always wondered about this idea of God hardening Pharaoh's heart. I just automatically assumed that this poor ruler was getting stomped upon by God. Just when he was ready to let the people go, God hardens his heart for another round of plagues. Where is the fairness in that? Where is the free will? Hardening Pharaoh's heart suggested to me that just when Pharaoh decided to let the people go, God jumped in and said, "No, you will not, either. I am going to make you suffer, and there is nothing you can do about it. I will force My will upon you and make it so you do not let these people go. How do you like them apples?"

I discovered the Jewish approach to this question is far different than that of the Christian. In fact, it flows to the very heart of our approach to our own faith. The very conclusion that the Jews reach on this matter flies in the face of our Christian evangelistic efforts and our Western "me first" culture.

Before I ever met my first rabbi, I was led to believe that the Jews do not believe in heaven or hell. This is not true; they do believe in an afterlife. Even when they give a toast they will often declare the afterlife exists when they say *"l'chaim,"* which means, to life. The word is in a plural form and suggests not only our natural life but our other life—that is, our spiritual and eternal life.

The reason Christians feel the Jews do not believe in a heaven or hell is because they never talk about the afterlife. Their focus is on their life here and now. Their mission on earth is to follow the greatest commandment. This commandment is recited in their daily *shema* or confession—"Thou shalt love the Lord thy God with all thy heart." In the New Testament, Jesus even confirms this in Mark 12:33, *"And to love him with all the heart, and with all the understanding, and with all the soul, and with all the strength, and to love his neighbour as himself, is more than all whole burnt offerings and sacrifices."* This speaks of the Jewish mission in life, which is to love God with all your heart, soul, and might, and to love your neighbor as yourself. This is their focus.

They deliberately avoid talking about the afterlife for a very good reason. As one rabbi explained to me, to talk about the afterlife, as Christians do, tends to make our purpose in life merely a preparation for the afterlife. If they occupy themselves with the afterlife, then they fear they will find themselves serving God and others in order to obtain their berth in a heavenly home and not because they love God or their neighbor. They believe that they will seek to love God and their neighbor only to earn a reward from God.

The Jews have faced generations of persecutions, hatred, and even attempted genocide. Yet, they have remained true to their mission to love God with all their hearts, souls, and might and to love their neighbors as themselves, without ever mentioning the idea that rewards await those who are faithful.

Does God need to hold a gun to our heads or threaten us with torment in eternal fires to get us to follow Him? Does He have to bribe us or entice us with gifts of prosperity, healings, and a bag full of goodies to get us to give a tithe or teach a Sunday school class? Does He have to strike fear in our hearts to keep us in line lest we break one of His commandments and end up in that other place?

The Jews do not think so. When they read the book of Job, they do not focus on the last chapter where Job is rewarded with twice what was taken from him as many Christians do. They focus on Job's words, *"Though he slay me, yet will I trust in him: but I will maintain mine own ways before him"* (Job 13:15). Some translations say "hope" rather than "trust." In the Hebrew the word is *yachal*, which means to expect progress. I can see how they get the idea of hope as there is a sense of expectation, but that expectation is to make progress. The verse could read: "Though he slay me, yet I expect to progress in Him." What progression was Job looking for from his troubles? Obviously, if he were slain by God, there would be no benefit in the physical realm so it must be a spiritual benefit. I should note that the word *yachal* is in a Piel form which intensifies the verb so Job was saying that he had the expectation of a great and wonderful progression—if God slayed him, it would bring him into eternity to be joined as one with God. This seems to be the same idea the apostle Paul had, *"For me to live is Christ, to die is gain"* (Philippians 1:21).

So, what does all this have to do with God hardening Pharaoh's heart? The word "harden" in Hebrew in Exodus 7:3 is *'aqesheh*, which means to be harsh, severe, and/or fierce. It also means to be stubborn. This verb is found in a Hiphal form, which means it is causative. Pharaoh's heart was not already stubborn, harsh, severe, or fierce; it was caused by God to become stubborn, harsh, severe, or fierce. God would do this through the plagues He would send.

The Devil 87

Now after the final plague in Exodus 17:8, we find that the word that is used in Hebrew for "hardening" is *chazaq* and means to strengthen. This verb is in a Piel form, which is intensive. God fiercely strengthened Pharaoh's heart. In verse 17 we learn God also *chazaq* the hearts of the Egyptian army.

In Exodus 7:3 God caused the heart of Pharaoh to be harsh, severe, fierce, and stubborn. Pharaoh questioned, *"Who is the Lord, that I should obey his voice to let Israel go? I know not the Lord, neither will I let Israel go."* (Exodus 5:2). Pharaoh asked a legitimate question. "Who is the Lord?" After the tenth plague, God no longer needed to make Pharaoh's heart 'aqesheh (stubborn); he knew quite well who the Lord God Jehovah was by that time. After the tenth plague Pharaoh had reached decision time and so God had to *chazaq*, strengthen Pharaoh's heart. This is where God needed to do something to make sure Pharaoh's heart was not influenced by the ten plagues.

Nachmanides, also referred to by the acronym Ramban, was a leading medieval Jewish scholar, Bible commentator, and Hebrew master. His writings provide a straightforward explanation for why God hardened Pharaoh's heart. However, you need to understand the Jewish mindset to understand Nachmanides' answer as to why God *chazaq* the heart of Pharaoh. If God did not harden Pharaoh's heart, He would have deprived him of the ability to make a coherent and true choice. He would not be able to exercise his free will. The plagues would compel Pharaoh to let the people of God leave Egypt because God was putting a gun to his head and hence his decision to let the people go would not be truly one of free choice. It would be like a robber putting a gun to your head and saying, "Give me the keys to your car." You would hand them over not because of any love between you and the crook but because you had no choice, other than being shot. That robber is also robbing you of your free will. God does not believe in a shotgun wedding. If Pharaoh was to give his heart to God, God wanted him to do it out of respect, honor, and love; not out of fear. From a Christian standpoint, fear is a tool of the enemy. God only operates out of love.

God had demonstrated who and what He was and now it was time for Pharaoh to make a decision. Would he follow God or not? If he followed God, was it because God held a gun to his head? In our Western Christian thinking we shake our heads and say, "That crazy Pharaoh, he would rather die and go to hell than submit to God." I do not believe Pharaoh was crazy; I believe he was blinded by God. The blinders that God put on Pharaoh were to hide all the plagues, remove the fear that was in him so that he could make a rational and coherent decision based on whether he would admit in his heart there was a true God out there, a God more powerful that he was. He had to choose to love or reject Him, bow to this God Jehovah or dismiss Him and continue to be his own god. If he were to choose God, recognize Him as his creator and bow to Him, it would not be because God put a gun to his head. It would be because he truly wanted to serve God Jehovah and learn to love Him with all his heart, soul, and might.

Recently in the news, there was the revelation of a scandal where a candidate for a political office was offered any job she wanted and/or a large amount of money if she would withdraw from the campaign. This candidate responded that no amount of money would persuade her to withdraw. She was in the race to serve her country and not to get an important job or gain wealth. We could say her heart was *chazaq*, strengthened or hardened against any outside influence such as wealth or power. Her focus remained on serving her people and by her refusal of the bribe, she proved she had the right motive to serve in that office she was seeking.

Pharaoh would have readily accepted God's efforts to recognize Him as his Creator and follow Him to save his own gizzard so he would not suffer any other plagues. But God wanted to be loved not feared, so God had to *chazaq*, to strengthen, Pharaoh's true motive for letting God's people go. He had to blind him to the effects of the plague to allow him to make a rational decision whether to bow before God or not. Pharaoh's decision was to be based not upon fear but upon a recognition of his Creator and his desire to learn to love Him or reject His loving advances.

I still personally believe that the enemy is a sentient being and that there are demonic forces out there wreaking havoc in the world. But I have no problem incorporating the Jewish belief of a *yetzar hara'*, an inclination to evil or, as we Christians would call it, a sinful nature. However, even though I do not believe He created a subservient angel who was designed for the specific role of seducing us away from God, that concept has given me insight into understanding why God allows us to have a sinful nature. It is there to complete the circle of free will. If such an angel did exist, I would be grateful God created such a being because it would give me an opportunity to choose God, to choose to love Him. The *hasatan*, or sinful nature, empowers me to bring a special joy to the God of the universe that no other creature can bring. I can choose to love God and it is that free choice of choosing God over the impulses of my sinful nature that brings Him the joy He so longs for. It explains why He created this human creature in the first place.

I do not fear the powers of a *hasatan* or his minions for I have free will to reject the seduction of the *yetzar hara'*, whether it is a sentient being or just an evil inclination. I just know I have a choice, a free will, and if I choose to follow God, I will cause that *yetzar hara'* or *hasatan* to 'erag or flee in pain and torment. With this opportunity or challenge, it only serves to give me the joy of choosing to reject that seduction to demonstrate my love for my Creator.

I have the opportunity to experience a joy that even the angels could not experience. An opportunity to bring a joy to God that no other created beings without free will can bring to God, and that is to choose to love Him.

12

THE NATIVITY

*"And she brought forth her firstborn son, and wrapped him
in swaddling clothes, and laid him in a manger;
because there was no room for them in the inn. And there
were in the same country shepherds abiding in the field,
keeping watch over their flock by night."*
—Luke 2:7–8

*"And thou, O tower of the flock, the strong hold of the
daughter of Zion, unto thee shall it come,
even the first dominion; the kingdom shall come to the
daughter of Jerusalem."*
—Micah 4:8

If there is something very ironic in regard to my study of Judaism through the lenses of a Christian biblical language teacher, it is that I developed a whole new understanding and appreciation for the Christmas story. It is ironic because Jews do not accept Jesus as

92 *What the Rabbis Know That I Never Learned in Church*

the Messiah and yet the whole story of Jesus and His birth could not be more Jewish. There were many things in the Christmas story that did not make much sense to me before I started studying the works of rabbis, learning about Jewish culture, and reading Jewish literature. Suddenly, it was like I was putting together a jigsaw puzzle with the missing pieces I found buried deep within the Talmud, Mishnah, and other Jewish works.

So let me start with what "nativity" means. The word itself is not found in the Bible. It comes from the Latin verb *nacsi* meaning birth, and it eventually evolved into the Latin word *nativitas*, which means to be born.

Our story opens in the Gospels. Let's begin with Matthew 1:18. We find Mary the mother of Jesus is espoused (engaged or betrothed) to Joseph. We know very little about Joseph other than he was espoused to Mary. We picture him from all the phony movies and pictures as a young man about Mary's age, most likely in his late teens and of course quite handsome.

That is the first thing that raises some red flags as to the accuracy of this depiction. We find that Joseph made some mature, independent decisions that under Jewish tradition should have involved his parents. This is a sure sign that Joseph was quite a bit older than Mary and may have even been a widower. To make the decision to quickly divorce Mary likely would not have occurred as an independent decision if this were his first marriage. Mary was still a virgin so this would be her first marriage, and she would likely have been around fourteen years of age. Normally a young girl was considered of marriageable age when she reached puberty. Joseph could have been well into his twenties and even thirties. Such age differences were not unusual, even today in many parts of the world.

Note carefully what we find in John 2:3–4 where Jesus performed His first miracle at a wedding by turning water into wine. This was before He even started his ministry.

*And when they wanted wine, the mother of Jesus saith unto
him, they have no wine. Jesus saith unto her, Woman, what
have I to do with thee? mine hour is not yet come.*

It sounds so disrespectful for Jesus to call his mother "woman."
However, in Aramaic, Jesus used the word *'anath*. In that culture,
by calling His mother *'anath*, He was really showing a sign of
respect. This presents the best case that Joseph had died before
Jesus began His ministry. *'Anath* was a word used for a single
mother who, after the death of her husband, had raised her children under the hardship of widowhood. We have no English word
for *'anath*. It is an Aramaic term of endearment that could have
many possible renderings in English, none which could render justice to the Aramaic word. I believe the NIV has the best possible
English equivalent of *"dear woman."* We can only say that it is a
tender, respectful response. For Jesus to have used the word *'anath*
would suggest that Mary entered widowhood while Jesus was still
a child. It is suggested that Joseph was likely twice the age of Mary
when they were married.

Joseph and Mary were espoused, that is betrothed. In Jewish
teaching if one were betrothed, they were essentially bound
together as much as if they had already been legally married, only
they could not live together or have a sexual relationship for at
least a year. Marriages were arranged, and many times the bride
and bridegroom had not even met until their wedding day. Hence,
before they were allowed to be intimate physically, they were given
a year to become intimate emotionally.

The idea was that the couple would be legally married, but
the bride would still live with her parents while the bridegroom
prepared a place for her to live with him. This would usually be
an attachment to the bridegroom's father's house. *"In my Father's
house are many mansions: if it were not so, I would have told you. I go
to prepare a place for you. And if I go and prepare a place for you, I*

will come again, and receive you unto myself; that where I am, there ye may be also" (John 14:2–3). In these verses Jesus is illustrating our relationship with Him is like a betrothal period while we live on earth. We are legally married to Jesus when we accept Him as our personal Savior but the marriage is not consummated until He returns to take us to His Father's house in heaven.

This arrangement of a betrothal would last for about a year. After that time of being together emotionally but not physically, the bridegroom would long for a deeper, intimate physical relationship, to be completed or joined with his bride. Finally, one day when he could no longer be separated from his beloved, he would come to his father-in-law's house late at night to snatch away his bride and take her to his father's house to consummate the marriage. Neighbors and friends would watch anxiously at night, waiting for that evening when the bridegroom comes after his bride and then they would all come out of their houses and form a procession as the bridegroom carries his bride to his father's house and consummates the marriage. While this consummation is going on in the *yichud* room or tent, there would be a big party taking place. This is alluded to in Matthew 25:1–13, the story of the foolish virgins who did not have oil for their lamps, and when the bridegroom came they were unable to attend the wedding feast.

This, however, does not seem to the case with Mary and Joseph. An older man who was a widower would not be required to go through a yearlong betrothal. A couple weeks or no waiting period at all would be acceptable for an older, formerly married man.

To avoid any scandal when the pregnancy was revealed to Joseph, once he got the go-ahead from the angel, he took Mary right away into his home. (See Matthew 1:19–24.) Normally first-century Jewish women would not reveal that they were pregnant until five months into the pregnancy. Following this tradition, it would have given Joseph enough time to immediately bring

Mary into his already established home and live with her. When the time of pregnancy was announced, people would just assume Joseph was the father.

This leads me to believe that Joseph was a widower. As a widower he could take his new bride into his house any time after the betrothal ceremony. Normally, there would not be a feast for a second marriage, unless the bride specially requested it.

To take Mary to Bethlehem for the census would also indicate that they had a shortened betrothal period and that Joseph was established as an independent man, again an indication that he was a widower.

There are a number of laws that Jewish women follow when pregnant. One law is that a pregnant woman is not to look or gaze upon an unkosher animal. All these nativity scenes with camels and donkeys are highly inaccurate, as the camel and donkey are not kosher. We assume the wise men arrived on camels, although donkeys were the favored form of desert travel in the first century. We find in Matthew 2:11, *"And when they were come into the house, they saw the young child with Mary his mother."* The verse does not mention Joseph. Now there are many who believe the wise men showed up many months after Jesus was born because the trip from out West would have taken many months. But why could the star to guide them not appear many months before the birth so they arrived just after the birth took place? The other argument for a delayed appearance is that in Matthew the Greek word used for the baby is *paidion,* which is a word for a young child, not an infant. But in Aramaic the word used is *tela',* which is a word for a young child that is also used for an infant. Interestingly, it is also a word used for a little lamb, which is metaphorically what Jesus was born to be; that is, a lamb who would be sacrificed.

So where was Joseph? It is a little strange that they found the *tela'* with his mother but it does not mention the father. Again, some say Joseph died, which is not likely as Mary gave birth to a number of other children and here Jesus is still very young. In fact, they are still in Bethlehem. At least that is what Scripture teaches. Then we could say Joseph was running errands when the wise men arrived, although I hardly think Joseph would have left Mary's side so soon after giving birth.

Another possibility is that under the laws for pregnant women, a husband is not allowed in the same room as his wife when she gives birth. So, the arrival of the wise men could have been timed perfectly for the moment of birth. This would be the purpose of the wise men showing up to witness the birth of the Messiah. If they were wise men from Persia, they would have been trained in delivering babies. But I think there was a more likely group of individuals who would have been more appropriate for this task, as I will explain later.

Once the child is born, the mother is to offer a *HaGamal* or a prayer of praise or blessing. This was to be done before ten relatives. However, if no relatives were around, she could say this blessing before ten Jewish men. I will also explain that one later as well.

Now tradition also teaches that there was no room in the inn for Joseph and Mary and they had to settle for a stable, a cave, or as often depicted in a nativity scene a three-sided flimsy lean-to. They put the baby Jesus in a manger, or as we would know it in the Western world, a feeding trough. This was to show His humble birth. However, recent archaeological discoveries, as well as an examination of the Talmud, would indicate that there are a couple things historically and culturally inaccurate with this picture.

The picture we have in our mind of a nativity scene is a little stable with a wooden manger filled with straw and all sorts of farm animals surrounding the baby. There would be three wise men and maybe three or four shepherds with Mary holding the baby and Joseph standing next to her. Such a shelter or stable did not really exist in the first century. It could have been a little succoth, which was a booth-type structure temporary set up during the time of planting or harvest. But these were temporary and were usually in a state of collapse by the time they were abandoned.

Then there is this wooden manger. It is very unlikely that this manger would be made of wood because farm animals like to chew on wood. Whoever owned this manger would have had to make it out of stone. Such mangers were not common in Israel. The only place you would find a manger would be in the Tower of the Flock or the *Migdal Eder*.

In reading the Talmud, I found something interesting. In Baba Kamma 80a and 7a,b, we learn that the fields of Eder, which is just a few feet from bordering Bethlehem, is where the sacrificial lambs were raised and cared for. The shepherds of these lambs were elite shepherds from the priestly tribe of Levi, tasked with ensuring the lambs remained without blemish or spot. They watched these sheep twenty-four hours a day. From birth, the little lamb would be spoiled rotten, fed a special diet, and wrapped in fine linen to remain without blemish or spot.

We learn from Scripture that Mary and Joseph were forced to spend the night in a location other than an inn because the inns were all full. The Aramaic text, however, does not even mention an inn, stating instead *dalith hu lahun dukath*—there was no place for them. Inns in those days were not what we think. They were little way places that were built in a circle or square and had two stories. The bottom had feed troughs for the camels, donkeys, or other livestock. The second floor was where the travelers slept. In the center, there was a well and a number of campfires that people shared. It was very communal, and dangerous. There were no innkeepers to keep order. These inns were established because the roads were filled with bandits and you might wake up and find your camels or donkeys stolen. However, you stood a better chance of waking up in the morning with your livestock and supplies (as well as your life) if you stayed in one of these inns. Should you have done what tradition teaches—that Mary and Joseph supposedly slept in a stable or cave that served as a feeding area for livestock—you were placing yourself at extreme risk from undesirables. Yet, even if they did stay at such an inn, these places were not entirely safe. There was still a chance you would wake up to find your livestock and supplies gone. The inn was not the best place for a pregnant Jewish woman, as there were many animals in the inn that would not be kosher.

As I indicated earlier, a manger would only be found in a place like in the Tower of the Flock or the *Migdal Eder* where the sheep were pampered and given a very strict diet as they were the sacrificial lambs. This is where the lambs who were to be used for the temple sacrifice would be born.

> And this shall be a sign unto you; Ye shall find the babe wrapped in swaddling clothes, lying in a manger.
>
> (Luke 2:12)

Now how would this be a sign if swaddling clothes and mangers were common in the first century? Actually, swaddling was not a common practice among the Jews. The fabric for swaddling was expensive and not all could afford such luxuries. But swaddling was a practice in the Tower of the Flock where a newborn lamb that was to be a sacrificial lamb was cared for. The newborn lambs were placed in a manger, which I indicated earlier would have been made of stone. It was carefully cleaned, and the newborn lamb was carefully examined and wrapped in swaddling clothes, white linens, which would be used to **find and protect the newborn lamb from any blemishes.** As we know, the sacrificial lambs had to be without spot or blemish and these priestly shepherds took much care to make sure that the lambs were free of any infirmities. They would use the finest linen. Only the wealthy could afford fine linen, at least linen that was not coarse but fine enough to wrap a baby in. The high priest normally would wear this type of linen. If Jesus was born in the Tower of the Flock, it is only reasonable that He was wrapped in the fine linen used for the sacrificial lambs.

Hence this was an excellent sign to the shepherds. I mean Bethlehem was a large enough town that a door-to-door search would have taken days to find the newborn Jesus. But when the angel said that the baby was wrapped in swaddling clothes laying in a manger, these shepherds knew right where to go, for they were likely shepherds who were guarding the temple sheep. They would go right to the *Migdel Eder* or the Tower of the Flock.

Many Bible scholars believe Micah 4:8 predicts where the birth of the Messiah would take place. The Talmud predicts that the Messiah would be born in a castle. That really depends on how you translate the Aramaic word for "castle." It is the word *migdel*, which could also mean a tower or a place of height or high honor. Dubious as it may seem, it was a place of high honor for the lambs, for only the best, purest, and cleanest lambs without blemish or spot were born in this castle, the *Migdel Eder* or the Tower of the Flock. A quick Internet search for *Migdel Eder* results in pictures that resemble a castle.

"And there were in the same country shepherds abiding in the field, keeping watch over their flock by night" (Luke 2:8). In Aramaic the word "country" is *'athra*, which means region, place, or location. It could be miles or just a few feet away.

There is debate among preachers as to why the shepherds were alerted to the birth of the Messiah. That is a good question, but the answer is easily found in the Talmud. For one thing, if Jesus were indeed born in the *Migdel Eder*, it would be reasonable to assume that the shepherds who received the announcement were priestly shepherds. It is more correct that they were the Levitical shepherds. Although the Levites were the priestly tribe, not all Levites were functioning priests. Functioning priests—those who were of the direct line of Aaron—carried out the ceremonial duties of the temple including the sacrifices. Those Levites who were not of the lineage of Aaron would be the ones to maintain and take care of the temple, temple choir, raising of the sacrificial lambs, and so on.

Thus, the shepherds were not dirty, lowlife, ex-criminal types, as often depicted by many preachers, and the angels did not appear to them to show that God cared for the lowlifes. These were highly trained elite shepherds. They were the veterinarians of their day, skilled not only in how to care for sheep but how to deliver a newborn lamb. Just as a newborn sacrificial lamb was brought into this world by these priestly shepherds, we too can assume that the sacrificial lamb of God was brought into this world by the same shepherds.

So why were these shepherds summoned by the angel? Well, according to Jewish custom, the mother of a newborn child would offer a blessing called a *HaGamel*. However, this blessing had to be done before ten relatives. If there were not ten relatives close by then ten male Jews could be summoned to receive this blessing. So, these shepherds were summoned to form a *minyan* or the quorum of ten, which was the minimum number to be present for this blessing and for the worship that would follow.

> *And when they were come into the house, they saw the young child with Mary his mother, and fell down, and worshipped him: and when they had opened their treasures, they presented unto him gifts; gold, and frankincense, and myrrh.*
>
> (Matthew 2:11)

The identity of the wise men in this Matthew account is uncertain. Matthew only tells us that they came from the East or in a literal translation of the Greek *from the rising (of the sun)*. It is believed by many that they came from Persia, as they were called *magi*. This word comes from the Old Persian word *magus* and the Aramaic word *magusah*, which is a reference to the priest of a Zoroastrian cult that was pantheistic and studied astrology. Some scholars believe they were sages from India and others, as

Chrysostom, believe they were from Yemen as the kings of Yemen were Jewish. A recent discovery of a document in an old dialect of Aramaic speaks of a religious order devoted to private prayer in an unknown land called Shir that believed God would be born as a human and His birth would be announced by an unusually bright star.

One thing we can be sure of, however, is that they were either Jewish or had a great affinity toward the Jewish God Jehovah. They were also very knowledgeable of Jewish worship for their gift of gold, frankincense, and myrrh contained the three key elements in Jewish worship.

The time of their appearing is highly debated. Many believe that because Herod ordered the death of all children under the age of two that Jesus was likely two years old when the wise men showed up. Some point to the Greek word *paidon*, which is rendered as young child as evidence that Jesus had to be at least two years old when the wisemen arrived. As explained earlier *paidon* is a word for young child but not an infant. The word in Greek for an infant is *brephos*. However, the word in Aramaic is *tela'*, which is the word for a little lamb. Since Matthew spoke Aramaic and not Greek, he would have used the word *tela'* when he gave the inspired text and the scribe translating the word knew there was no Greek word for *tela'* so he settled on using *paidon*. If we follow the Aramaic text, the argument for the use of the Greek word *paidon* would not hold up. To say it took two years to follow the star is assuming that the star first appeared at the birth of Jesus, but how do we know it did not appear over Bethlehem at the moment of the birth? Yet, it could have appeared two years earlier, moved across the skies for a two year period until it settled over Bethlehem.

I would argue that the appearance over Bethlehem at the time of the birth is significant because the wisemen came to worship the newborn. Unless ten wise men were present there would not have been a minyan (a quorum of ten) to carry on this worship. They may have relied on the presence of the shepherds to conduct their worship service. That brings us to the question of the gifts.

Reading this story in the *Pershitta*, the Aramaic Bible, I discovered something very interesting about these gifts. For one thing, there was only one gift. The Aramaic word used for *gift* is *qorbana*. This word is in a singular form and ends with a definite article; hence it would be rendered, *they presented Him with **the** gift*. But this word being rendered as *gift* is very misleading. It comes from the word *qorban*, the word Jesus used in Matthew 15:6 where He rebukes the Pharisees for calling their offering a *qorban*. A *corban* is literally an offering or sacrifice to God. It could be an animal sacrifice or an incense offering, which was most likely the case here. The word *corban* comes from a Semitic root that has its origins in the Akkadian word *QRB*, which means to draw close to someone. It evolved into the meaning of *offering* or *gift* as the intent of the offering or gift is to bring you closer to the receiver. Thus, the purpose of the *incense offering* was to bring you closer to God. The gift paralleled the gift of God in giving His only begotten Son, who came to earth for the primary purpose of bringing humankind closer to God.

Frankincense or myrrh were used only in the holy of holies and were mixed in a golden vessel and burned on a golden plate. Actually, the Talmud teaches that the term "frankincense and myrrh" represented a combination of essential oils/incense but to avoid listing all the oils, the incense or oil was given the name of the primary oil that was used. Frankincense was the primary oil, which had stacte, onycha, and galbanum added. Myrrh was the primary oil with the addition of aromatic bark, cassia, and cinnamon added (Talmud, Kritut 6A). Exodus 30:33–37 warns that these compounds are not to be used outside of the holy of holies and are not for anyone other than God, lest they be cut off from the people. When the high priest entered the holy of holies and burned these incenses, it was said that God's presence appeared in the midst of the vapors. The people outside the holy of holies would know that God's presence was there because they would smell the incense. I had a friend who told me that when she worshipped God in her car, one time she suddenly smelled this sweet fragrance. Her sister, also in the car, claimed not to really smell it, but my friend did. I think what she smelled was that fragrance that the Hebrews associated with the presence of God.

It developed throughout the history of the tabernacle and later temple that some came to believe that burning such incense would summon the presence of God, but Amos cleared that up in Amos 5:21 where he said, "*I hate, I despise your feast days, and I will not smell in your solemn assemblies.*" The word "smell" is 'arich, which comes from the root word rauch, which means spirit but is also used for an aroma. In the context where it is used, it is most likely a play on the Aramaic word 'arak, which has the idea of restoration or healing. This appears to be a direct reference to the incense burned in the holy of holies and God is saying that He despises these incenses when they are offered without sincerity as the Israelites were doing it. Instead, it was being offered only to draw the presence of God so they could get some goodies like a healing or restoration. In other words, they were burning the incense to call upon God or to entice or bribe God to solve their problems and to draw closer to Him, not to use it as a *corban*. God is literally saying, you cannot conjure Me up by burning incense.

Yet, there was a purpose for using the incense, frankincense, and myrrh in worship as it was commanded by God. It was used as a *qorban*, an offering to draw near to God. This was what the wise men presented to Jesus. That is why I believe people like my friend have smelled a fragrance while worshipping God because God may just use that fragrance to draw them closer to Him. The word in Aramaic used for "present" is *qeren*, which also has a Semitic root meaning to present an offering or sacrifice to draw near. It has almost the same meaning as *qorbana*. Thus the wise men did not *present unto Him gifts,* but in the Aramaic Bible it could be rendered as *they drew near to Him with their incense sacrifice or their qorban.*

But note that they were not in the holy of holies when they offered this *qorban,* which is in direct violation of Exodus 30. Or was it? Was not the holy of holies the place where the presence of God rested? Thus, there in that little manger, not the holy of holies, these wise men combined the sacred oils and incense in golden vessels before the baby Jesus, the very presence of God. They then burned the oils and incense on golden plates and worshipped God as the High Priest did in the holy of holies. Were the wise men ushering in a new age of worship? This worship needed no human high priest; it was a worship that everyone could perform. When Jesus died on the cross, the veil separating the holy of holies was ripped apart and now we all have access to the very presence of God through our new High Priest, Jesus Christ.

Oh, and the third element to the worship, gold? Everything in the holy of holies was to be made of pure gold. You see, ancient man discovered that gold had a property that no other metal had. All other metals that you hold in your hand will grow warm, except gold. Gold will remain cool, passive, and aloof, like the gods. Thus, it was believed that gold was the skin of the gods. All idols were made of gold, the skin of the gods, and they worshipped the gold or the skin of the gods. But the Hebrews merely used this gold or what the pagans believed to be the skin of their gods to service the true God Jehovah, to mix His oils and incense on the platform made of the skin of pagan god, using it as a base to burn the incense of the true God.

You see the gold, frankincense, and myrrh were not the gifts given by the wise men. They burned up the frankincense and myrrh and they most likely took the golden cups and plates home with them to continue to burn their oils and worship God. Mary and Joseph didn't take the oils and the gold and sell it for passage to Egypt as that was not the gift that the magi gave to Jesus. *The Gift of the Magi* was a hazardous journey untaken for only one purpose found in Matthew 2:2, *"we...are come to worship Him."* The *Gift of the Magi* is the only gift that is acceptable to God, the only gift other than our very lives we can truly give to God this Christmas and that is to **worship Him.**

> *Sanctify unto me all the firstborn, whatsoever openeth the womb among the children of Israel, both of man and of beast: it is mine.* (Exodus 13:2)

> *And when the days of her purification according to the law of Moses were accomplished, they brought him to Jerusalem, to present him to the Lord; (As it is written in the law of the* LORD, *Every male that openeth the womb shall be called holy to the Lord;) And to offer a sacrifice according to that which is said in the law of the Lord, A pair of turtledoves, or two young pigeons.* (Luke 2:22–24)

The story of Anna and Simeon is a very important addition to the Christmas story as it explains something many have often wondered about. If Jesus was from the tribe of Judah, how could he be a priest or high priest? I have heard this story of how Simeon blessed Jesus many times, but no one bothers to explain the Jewish tradition behind this interlude to the Christmas story before Mary and Joseph fled to Egypt. In fact, they leave out this very important point to this Christmas story so often that I never heard it explained concerning Jesus's consecration as a priest.

After the days of purification ended, Mary and Joseph brought the baby to Jerusalem to present Jesus to the Lord. This ritual that took place in the temple in Jerusalem is called *Pidyon Haben* or the redemption of the son. This was a ceremony where the father of the first-born male redeems his son from the priesthood by giving five silver coins to a priest who is a direct descendent of Aaron thirty days after the baby's birth. This would ceremonially pass on the eldest's duties as a priest to a Levite priest. This law was enacted prior to the establishment of the priestly lines. Up to that point, the eldest took the role of a priest. Once the Aaronic line was established, this ritual of *pidyan haden* was performed before a Levitical priest who would symbolically assume the child's duties as priest and the five pieces of silver would redeem him from his obligation. This ritual serves as a reminder that God is the owner of all things, including the best and first that you have. This is what the Scripture in Exodus means when it says the eldest belongs to God. Just as Jephthah's vow said he would give to the Lord or offer up as a burnt offer who or whatever walked through his door. "Give to the Lord" was a phrase meaning the person would serve in the temple or tabernacle for the rest of their lives. Jephthah's daughter walked through and he was bound to give her to the Lord, that is, she was to serve in temple all her life like Anna in Luke 2 or Samuel in 1 Samuel.

According to Exodus, the first-born child belongs to God and the father is to redeem him with five pieces of silver. Only Scripture says that Mary and Joseph offered two turtle doves or two pigeons, the offering of a poor person. But wait, why just a sacrifice?

That is how Jesus, who was not a member of the priestly line, could be a priest. Mary and Joseph were not going to redeem Him with five pieces of silver; they were going to consecrate Him with the sacrifice of the doves and pigeons. Thanks to Mary, Joseph, and a godly priest named Simeon, Jesus was not redeemed from the duties of a priest but was consecrated to become our priest, and not just a priest but our High Priest.

Thus, we find in the Christmas story that the Messiah was not only born in a castle, but was also born to be a sacrificial lamb who would die for our sins, and would also become our High Priest.

13

THE GOVERNMENT WILL BE UPON HIS SHOULDER

"For unto us a child is born, unto us a son is given:
and the government shall be upon his shoulder: and his name
shall be called Wonderful Counsellor, The mighty God,
The everlasting Father, The Prince of Peace."
—Isaiah 9:6

With the advent of worship teams, church choirs are starting to become an endangered species, if they are not already extinct in most churches. That is good and bad in certain ways. With the passing of church choirs we have the demise of Christmas and Easter Cantatas. I really do not have any fond memories of the cantatas that I was forced to sit through as a child—not that they were of no value but as a restless eight-year-old child, I usually had to endure these musical performances rather than enjoy them. Hence, I have little to no recollection of even the titles of the

108 *What the Rabbis Know That I Never Learned in Church*

numerous cantatas I sat through. However, there is one musical score that I just can't get out of my head. It is a musical version of Isaiah 9:6 and the phrase, *"And the government shall be upon his shoulder."*

I guess I really needed a course in music appreciation but to an eight year old to hear, *"And the government shall be upon his shoulder,"* repeatedly was enough to drive any little kid to fidgeting. It wasn't enough to repeat it multiple times, but then they started to do it in a halting voice like some opera or bad movie musical. You know the routine where the choir emphasizes each syllable, "and the gov—er—ment—shall—be—," and so on; sort of like they hiccup their way through it. Not only would the whole choir perform together, but each vocal group would sing their respective parts, starting with tenors, then basses, altos, and sopranos. They finally work their way down to the pastor's wife singing it as a solo in her falsetto voice, making one wonder just how many tanks of helium were needed to get her through that song.

As an adult, I still lack a greater appreciation for cantatas since I never took that music appreciation class. Whenever I hear Isaiah 9:6, I relive in my mind that pastor's wife glitching her way through the song. I can't help but think, "What in the blazes does that mean anyway?" I have sat through numerous sermons where the preachers said it meant that the governments would be making things difficult for Jesus. I was satisfied with that explanation until I started to examine the context. Something so negative just did not fit the positive tone of that verse. I mean this verse starts off with something wonderful—*"unto us a child is born, unto us a son is given."* Then we learn that His name will be called Wonderful Counselor, Mighty God, Everlasting Father, Prince of Peace. But sandwiched in between these wonderful declarations is that negative thought that He would bear the weight of the government upon His shoulders. I was never really satisfied with that explanation,

The Government Will Be Upon His Shoulder 109

nor the more common explanation that the governments of this world would oppose Jesus and make His life miserable.

However, one day I had a rabbi explain it to me. It was not only the first time I heard an explanation that made sense to me, but I longed to hear that pastor's wife sing in falsetto her way through those words.

The rabbi explained that Christian translations of the Jewish Bible tend to do a lot of editorializing. Such is the case here with the Hebrew word *serah*, which is rendered as "government." In its Semitic root *serah* has the idea of protecting someone or fighting for someone. I checked this out through my personal resources and found that *serah* is not really a word for government. Instead, it is only somewhat connected, as the primary purpose of a government is to protect and fight for its citizens.

The phrase *thei hamaserahal shikemu*, which we render as *"the government shall be upon his shoulder,"* is an idiomatic expression that was used in the Near East in the climax of a marriage ceremony. Even today it is practiced in some Semitic cultures. However, it is a common practice in a Jewish wedding that is familiar to most of us. In a Jewish wedding ceremony, the bridegroom actually puts the veil on his bride's face to signify that although his bride is beautiful, he loves her and is marrying her for her inward beauty. As they age together and her outer beauty fades, he will still love her for her inward beauty. Removing the veil is the most dramatic and romantic moment of the wedding. The bride will walk around her groom three times declaring that she will teach him three things about God as found in Hosea 2:21–22. It is believed that the groom is closest to God during this time as his future wife's role will be to serve as a gateway to God. In fact, people often slip a prayer request to the bridegroom at this time to offer up to God.

It is believed that a male child receives instructions about the Torah, the laws of God, from his parents as he is going through childhood. When he becomes an adult and has mastered the laws of God, he is ready to leave his parents' instruction and be married to a woman who will replace his parents' role as teachers and take the role of instructing him in his love relationship to God. She will teach him of the love and mercy of God by loving him and being merciful to him. She will teach him of the righteousness and justice of God by being righteous and just before him. Finally, she will teach him of the faithfulness of God by being faithful to him.

She circles her bridegroom as the circle is the picture of eternity and thus, she is declaring that she will be betrothed to him forever to demonstrate what God promised to us in Hosea 2:19–20, *"And I will betroth thee unto me for ever; yea, I will betroth thee unto me in righteousness, and in judgment, and in lovingkindness, and in mercies. I will even betroth thee unto me in faithfulness: and thou shalt know the LORD."* Then the bridegroom will remove the veil from the bride's face and throw it over his shoulder. In this gesture the groom is making a public declaration that the government of his bride will be upon his shoulder. In other words, it will be his honor and privilege to now be her protector and provider. He will protect her heart and provide all the love and affection that God created her to desire, just as God has placed within us the need for love and affection from Him, which He has promised to provide. It is also a demonstration of the fact that we are to be God's protector and provider. That is to protect His heart and provide Him with all the love and affection that He longs for from us.

I believe that is what Isaiah 9:6 is conveying to us, not that the Messiah will have a difficult time with the governments of the earth. He will instead throw the veil of His bride over his shoulder signifying that He will be the protector and provider for His bride, which is each of us and His church. By dying on a cross and rising from the dead, He defeated the sin that keeps us from consummating our marriage to Him, and He will remove that veil from our face and throw it over His shoulder, signifying that He will protect our hearts and love us for all eternity.

Perhaps the good rabbi has given me an appreciation for the Christmas cantata after all as I could now sit and listen to a choir hiccup their way through the *and the gov—er—ment—will—be—* routine. For each time I hear those words, I would think of all the times in my life when Jesus was my protector and provider, a role He voluntarily took on because of His love for me.

14

THE THIRD TEMPLE

*"Thou shalt bring them in, and plant them in the mountain
of thine inheritance, in the place, O Lord,
which thou hast made for thee to dwell in, in the Sanctuary,
O Lord, which thy hands have established.
The Lord shall reign for ever and ever."*
—Exodus 15:17–18

*"I knew a man in Christ above fourteen years ago, (whether
in the body, I cannot tell; or whether out of the body, I
cannot tell: God knoweth;) such an one caught up to the third
heaven. And I knew such a man (whether in the body, or
out of the body, I cannot tell: God knoweth;) How that he
was caught up into paradise, and heard unspeakable words,
which it is not lawful for a man to utter."*
—2 Corinthians 12:2–4

*"And the temple of God was opened in heaven, and there was
seen in his temple the ark of his testament."*
—Revelation 11:19

> "Because very soon, when Moshiach (the Messiah) comes, we will experience these great expressions of love and connection with God. You will know and understand. All this will come with the Beit Hamiqadash (the third temple). However, it only becomes the Beit Hamiqadash (third temple) when it is completed and descends (from the heavens) with the coming of Moshiach (the Messiah) in the clouds."[3]
> —Menachem Mendel Schneerson

I am surprised to learn how few Christians know that back in 1948, when the United Nations was debating over creating a State of Israel, there was a strong contingent of Jews who opposed the establishment of the Jewish nation. Their reasoning was clear: only the Messiah could bring in the nation of Israel when He descended into the clouds. Further still, I am surprised that many Christians are unaware that the same contingent, who still oppose the establishment of Israel as a nation, also oppose the building of the third temple.

The reason behind that is just as clear. For one thing, it is believed that even before the building of the second temple, Ezekiel prophesied the building of another temple. There are a number of Scriptures that allude to the third temple or the *Beit Hamiqadash*. The word *beit* means house or place of dwelling, and the *Hamiqadash* comes from the root word *kodesh*, which means holy, with the definite article *Hei* for The Holy Place of Dwelling. During the days of Jesus, there was much debate over the legality of the second temple, and it came as no surprise to many when Jesus spoke of the temple's destruction. In fact, that is why He created such a disturbance when He spoke of it. Many zealots

---

3. Menachem Mendel Schneerson, *Torat Habayit, Sefer Hamaamarim 5689* (Sichos in English, 2015), 189.

of the Jewish faith plotted to destroy the temple, and when Jesus mentioned the destruction of the temple, He was automatically identified as one of these traitors.

The Samaritans were forbidden to worship in the second temple, but oddly, many were alright with that. The Samaritans were descendants of the Northern ten tribes of Israel who were left behind when the nation was taken into captivity by the Assyrians. During their time in captivity, they intermarried with foreigners, which was forbidden by Torah law. When the Jews returned from captivity, they viewed the Samaritans as heretics, and thus, they were forbidden to worship in the second temple. These Samaritans viewed the second temple as corrupt and not built according to God's plan nor established by the Messiah. They were content to worship in the temple they built on Mt. Gerizim. They believed this was where Moses had originally intended the Israelites to worship. Radical Samaritans would plot with ultra-orthodox Jews in Judea to destroy the temple in Jerusalem.

Pilate was well aware of the descension among the Jewish community and the extreme right-wing radicals in Judea who were plotting to destroy the temple because they felt it was illegitimate as it was not built by the Messiah. This is why Pilate was not too anxious to arrest Jesus. He considered Jesus, who came from Galilee, to be an ally of the Samaritans and the Roman government, who wanted to destroy the temple.

There was good reason for these hard feelings toward the second temple. The rebuilt temple was clearly outlined in Ezekiel 43, but the instructions for the next temple were incomplete. The Jews went ahead and built it anyway without the complete plans. The Talmud in Yoma 9b and Yoma 21b tell us something very interesting. There were five things in the first temple that were not in the second temple: the ark of the covenant, the *Shechinah* glory or presence of God, the fire from heaven, the Holy Spirit, and the Urim and the Thummim. The Talmud further teaches that after the death of the latter prophets, which would be Haggai, Zachariah, and Malachi, the Holy Spirit was removed from Israel. The Holy Spirit would not return until the Messiah was glorified.

I often wondered what John 7:39 meant, *"But this spake he of the Spirit, which they that believe on him should receive: for the Holy Ghost was not yet given; because that Jesus was not yet glorified."* What does it mean that Jesus was not yet glorified? According to what I have read in Jewish literature, the Messiah must suffer humiliation, pain, and some say even death and resurrection. Then He would be glorified when He ascends to heaven and is established on the throne of His kingdom. At this time the Holy Spirit will return to Israel and dwell in the third temple.

Jesus suffered humiliation, pain, death, and resurrection, and ten days after His resurrection, He ascended to heaven. Jesus died on Passover and fifty days after Passover is the Feast of Weeks. This is also known as Pentecost or the first fruits where the Jews celebrate the beginning of a new season with their produce and offer to God the first of their harvest as an offering. This first fruit could very well be a symbol of Jesus. This might explain why Jesus told His disciples to wait for the coming of the Holy Spirit. (See Luke 24:49.) Forty days after His ascension to heaven was the Feast of Pentecost, where the offering of the first fruits was accepted by God. Pentecost would have completed the glorification of Jesus and thus allowed the Holy Spirit to return.

We are all familiar with what happened in Acts 2:2–4:

And suddenly there came a sound from heaven, as of a rushing mighty wind, and it filled the whole house where they were sitting. Then there appeared to them divided tongues, as of fire, and one sat upon each of them. And they were all filled with the Holy Spirit and began to speak with other tongues, as the Spirit gave them utterance. (NKJV)

The Third Temple   117

Rabbinic teaching says that the Holy Spirit, the fire of God, and the prophetic power of the Urim and the Thummim would return to the temple. The second temple still stood, and these things did not return to the second temple. However, the apostle Paul does say that our bodies are the temple of God: *"What? know ye not that your body is the temple of the Holy Ghost which is in you, which ye have of God, and ye are not your own? For ye are bought with a price: therefore glorify God in your body, and in your spirit, which are God's"* (1 Corinthians 6:19–20). Our bodies are now the temple. When the Holy Spirit who dwelled in the temple returned, He returned to the temple, our bodies, which were made pure by the blood of Jesus the Messiah to allow for the indwelling of the Holy Spirit and the presence of God. When the presence of God that had rested upon the ark of the covenant returned, it returned to the temple, our bodies. When the Shechinah glory returned, it was to our bodies. The Spirit of God descended like tongues of fire, which could symbolically represent the fire of God. Could the speaking in tongues be the return of the prophetic power of the Urim and Thummim?

> *Charity never faileth: but whether there be prophecies, they shall fail; whether there be tongues, they shall cease; whether there be knowledge, it shall vanish away.*
>
> (1 Corinthians 13:8)

I grew up in a Baptist church where we were taught these spiritual gifts would cease. But it does not say that prophecies will cease; it says they will fail. The word used in the Greek for "fail" or "cease," as many modern translations render it, is *katargethesontai*, which comes from the root word *katargeo*, which means to bring to naught, abolish, annul, and make of no effect. In Aramaic, the word is *naphal*, which is actually a word used for an abortion; to bring a pregnancy to an end.

The Urim and Thummim were instruments that God used to speak to His people. Could we not be that instrument today? The Talmud teaches that the Urim and Thummim were the ephod worn by the high priest and the stones in the ephod represented not only the twelve tribes of Israel but also were used to represent the Hebrew alphabet, which would light up and spell out God's message. This was used by the high priest to determine the will of God, the direction of God, or the things my Charismatic friends often say when they prophesy over me.

Still, many Jews believed that there would be a third temple and that the Messiah would come to complete those portions of the temple not found in Ezekiel 43. They are arguing, even today, to wait for the Messiah before completing the third temple. In 515 BC, the Jews ignored the warning and instead of leaving the second temple uncompleted and awaiting the final instructions from the Messiah, they went ahead and built it according to the plans of the first temple.

The first temple was not built according the exact plans of God. Solomon used brass where he should have used gold, he purchased material from other nations when the material was supposed to be donated, and he built the temple on the backs of slave labor rather than volunteers. The temple is known today as Solomon's Temple and not God's Temple as Solomon built the temple as a memorial to himself. Ezekiel never gave the entire plans for the second temple, so it was not completed, as the Messiah was to come and give the final plans. However, the second was built according to the plans of the first temple. These plans were not accurate and then the temple was remodeled by King Herod, who established it as a monument to himself. Both temples were eventually destroyed.

Now today, once again, the Jews are pushing to rebuild the temple. However, they do not have the exact specifications for the third temple, the *Beit Hamiqadash*. If not built according to exact instructions, it will not serve as a Holy Place of dwelling for God.

Hence our bodies will continue to be that Holy Place or dwelling place for God.

We find something very interesting in 2 Corinthians 12:2–4. We have an account of Paul visiting the third heaven. The word in Aramaic for "heaven" is very similar to the Hebrew, yet has a shade of difference. It is the word *shami'a*, which means joyous, happy, and peaceful. It comes from the same root as *simchas*, which means rejoicing.

There is a teaching among Jews about seven levels of heaven, which I and other Christians do not believe and neither do many Jews. But we do have the apostle Paul saying he visited the third heaven? Among a strong segment of Jewish teachers, the third heaven is synonymous with the *Beit Hamiqadash*, the holy dwelling place of God or the third temple. As a good Jew and one who was trained in the depths of Jewish teaching, Paul was well aware of the expression of the third heaven as a reference to the true temple of God that was being prepared in the heavens. Those who rejected the second temple anticipated its destruction and that a third temple was being prepared in the heavens. Note that the word "heaven" is always found in a plural form in both Hebrew and Aramaic.

In the fourth verse Paul also visited paradise or *paradis* in Aramaic, which means a pleasure garden and is believed to be the abode of the righteous until the resurrection. It is considered a place of truth. In other words, the third heaven and paradise are two different places with the third heaven being the third temple. According to this Jewish teaching, when God recreates the earth, the third temple will descend to the earth, the garden of Eden will be revealed again, and the earth will transform back into the garden of Eden for all who are righteous—in Christian lingo those who have accepted Jesus as their Savior. This Jewish eschatology follows very closely to our Evangelical eschatology. We too believe the Messiah Jesus will return to earth, bringing the heavenly city where there will then be heaven on earth.

By the way, these Jews also believe that *paradis* is the garden of Eden, which exists in another realm. It exists alongside of us right now in another dimension like a parallel universe. It is where the righteous go after death. In Christian terms, we teach it is where those who have accepted Jesus as their Savior will go when they die, only we call it heaven.

Will the Jews build a third temple? They cannot build the third temple that will be a true holy dwelling place for God. Only the Messiah can build that temple, for only He will know the correct dimensions and style it is to be built. Now, there might come a someone who will convince the Jews he is the Messiah and will erect a temple. Beware, because if they successfully build a temple, they are not the Christ or Messiah, they are an anti-messiah or antichrist.

15

TRANSFIGURATION—TZIM TZUM

"Verily I say unto you, There be some standing here,
which shall not taste of death,
till they see the Son of man coming in his kingdom."
—Matthew 16:28

"And after six days Jesus taketh Peter, James,
and John his brother, and bringeth them up into an high
mountain apart, and was transfigured before them:
and his face did shine as the sun, and his raiment was white
as the light. And, behold, there appeared unto them Moses
and Elias talking with him."
—Matthew 17:1–3

It has always been a mystery to me as to what Jesus meant that some of His disciples would *"not taste of death till they see the Son of man coming in his kingdom."* I always assumed the coming of the Son of Man meant the second coming and His kingdom was the establishment of heaven on earth. That did not make sense as all the disciples did taste death and the second coming and the kingdom of God has yet to come.

There have been numerous explanations put forward, but none seemed to satisfy my personal curiosity. However, in my study of the teachings of rabbis, I believe I have found an explanation that does seem to fit this conundrum as to why some of the disciples would see the coming of the Son of Man before they taste death. That may be a reference to Peter, James, and John witnessing the transfiguration. That is, after all, what the very next verse after Matthew 16:28 talks about and could most likely be related.

The transfiguration itself has also been a mystery to me. I could never understand what that whole event was about until one day, I was reading Jewish literature and ran across something called *tzim tzum*. *Tzim tzum* literally means "reduction" and is a paradox of presence in absence. To really understand *tzim tzum* we need to go to the Old Testament and the story of the ark of the covenant.

I remember years ago, when I was working for Dr. Lester Sumrall's ministry, someone asked him a question concerning the location of the ark of the covenant. Rather than refer to the many references made by different preachers and teachers about the present location of the ark of the covenant, he just went to Scripture. He shared Revelation 11:19, "*The temple of God was opened in heaven, and there was seen in his temple the ark of his testament,*" which is another expression for the ark of the covenant. Thus, the ark of the covenant was in heaven.

I thought at the time that Dr. Sumrall was being very simplistic, but now, after many years of studying Jewish works, I am inclined to go along with his teaching. Jewish orthodox teaching tells us that the ark of the covenant is a "ghost covenant." According to the Talmud Yoma 21a, Megillah 10b, and Bava Batra 99a, the ark did not take up space. The holy of holies where the ark resided, was ten cubits wide, and the ark stood in the center. It had a length of 2.5 cubits. Yet, when measuring from the sides of the ark to the wall, it would measure five cubits on each side. Five cubits on either side added up to ten cubits. How do you fit the 2.5 cubits of the ark in the middle of that? The ark was both taking up space and not taking up space at the same time.

When the presence of God rested upon the ark, it was both in heaven and earth at the same time. That is called *tzim tzum*. It is present but not present at the same time. That is to say that the ark, when bearing the presence of God, was never really in this physical realm but was in the physical realm. If you can explain that, you can explain the Trinity. God bless you.

With quantum physics, we are closer to understanding *tzim tzum* when we consider the theories of alternative or multiple universes. The theory is that there are other universes or dimensions that exist alongside our universe. These are also known as parallel universes. There are unproven stories of people who slip into these alternative universes and wake up in the morning to discover everything is normal except for certain changes. For instance, a woman claims to have woken up one morning, went to work as she usually did, but found even though she worked in the same building, she occupied a different office and worked at a different job. Then, the next morning, she slipped back into her own universe again, where she was in her old office and job. There are numerous science fiction stories built on this theory, like the television series *Sliders*, about a young physics student who invents a wormhole that leads into other worlds similar to ours yet different. In these alternative worlds, he meets people who are really himself but in different roles. At one point, he meets his actual self from the future, who tells him he is about to experience great adventures. That would be an example of *tzim tzum*.

There are numerous explanations for the third heavens visited by the apostle Paul as I spoke about in a previous chapter. I would like to consider the *tzim tzum* as a plausible explanation. This

124 *What the Rabbis Know That I Never Learned in Church*

would be the area of heaven where the third temple exists. Rashi, the eleventh-century Jewish commentator and Hebrew master, claims in the Talmud in Sukkah 41a that the third temple has already been built and resides in the third heavens. Some individuals associated with the Temple Institute in Israel, an organization preparing to rebuild the third temple, dispute Rashi's interpretation of Exodus 15:17–18. These verses allegedly teach that God Himself will construct the third temple, which will be a permanent temple. Rashi teaches that it will be the Messiah under the direction of God that will build the third temple, but, of course, we as Christians believe Jesus is the Messiah and is God incarnate, so it is God Himself who has built the third temple. In other words, this particular group of Jews believe that the temple must not be built with human hands.

The apostle Paul claims to have made a visit to the third heaven and to paradise in 2 Corinthians 12:2–4. Some believe the third heaven and paradise are the same place, while others interpret them as two distinct locations. It is pure speculation, but you don't have to stretch the imagination too far to put this puzzle together to suggest that the third heaven is the resting place of the third temple.

Then we have the account of Revelation 11:19, which tells us that the temple is in heaven and the ark of the covenant is in this temple. Could this third heaven be in an alternative universe where the ark of the covenant dwells, and where the presence of God intersects with our natural realm in Revelation 11:19 in a sort of *tzim tzum*? To be fair and offer all sides, this is believed by dispensationalists to be just a vision. But then who is to say that a vision could not be a glimpse or portal into another universe, which Paul calls the third heavens?

Paul had been a member of the Sanhedrin and a Pharisee. He was a Jew among Jews and very immersed in Jewish traditions and teachings. The temple would have had great sentimental value to him and he knew that the second temple would be destroyed, not only from the teachings of Jesus, but just from the realization that the second temple was not built according to the exact design of God. Hence God taking him to the dimension or alternative universe where the third temple existed and was built by Messiah Jesus would have been a great comfort for him.

If the third temple is already in heaven with the ark of the covenant then how do you explain 2 Thessalonians 2:4?

Who opposeth and exalteth himself above all that is called God, or that is worshipped; so that he as God sitteth in the temple of God, shewing himself that he is God.

According to the popular dispensational viewpoint, the appearance of the Antichrist and the events described in the book of Revelation, as presented by Hal Lindsey, the "Left Behind" series, C. I. Scofield, and other pre-millennial teachers, are all considered future events. Therefore, it is believed that a temple in Israel must be built in the future. After all, if the Antichrist is to make a future appearance, he needs a temple to sit in. How can the third temple be on earth and in heaven at the same time?

Not that I am a dispensationalist and pre-millennialist, but I can see possible explanations. First, it could be *tzim tzum*. Second, according to 2 Thessalonians, the Antichrist will set himself up as God by sitting in the temple. That would mean that the antichrist would enter the holy of holies and sit on the ark of the covenant—that is not likely. Third, a temple will be built but it will not be the third temple. The ark of the covenant will be either discovered or remanufactured. If discovered, it would likely be a replica of the real ark, possibly discovered in some archeological dig and declared by so-called experts as authentic or remanufactured, featuring a mercy seat for the Antichrist. It would require a deception on the level of conspiracy theorists attempting to prove that the

126 *What the Rabbis Know That I Never Learned in Church*

moon landing was a fake, but I suppose it is possible, especially since the antichrist is believed to carry supernatural powers.

Maybe this would explain why Paul refers to his visit as a trip to the third heaven rather than the third temple because the final and permanent temple will not be the third temple but a fourth, as there will be another fake temple, a third temple that will be destroyed like the other two. The final temple will be massive. The second temple was only five hundred by five hundred cubits. The third temple will be three thousand by three thousand cubits. That is about 512 acres. This is about the size of the old Jerusalem, a city built with four squares. Perhaps that is what John is referring to as the *"holy city, the new Jerusalem."*

> *And I saw a new heaven and a new earth: for the first heaven and the first earth were passed away; and there was no more sea. And I John saw the holy city, the new Jerusalem, coming down from God out of heaven, prepared as a bride adorned for her husband.* (Revelation 21:1–2)

Then in Daniel 7:13 we find, *"I saw in the night visions, and, behold, one like the Son of man came with the clouds of heaven, and came to the Ancient of days, and they brought him near before him."* The Jews believe this verse in Daniel refers to the Messiah, who will come to earth in the clouds with the third and final temple.

Somehow, I see the concept of Jewish eschatology dovetailing with Christian eschatology. Dispensational Christianity teaches Jesus will return to earth with a new heaven and new earth. Jewish teaching shows that the Messiah will come to earth with the new Jerusalem or the new temple (the third temple).

So where is the ark of the covenant? It is in heaven, but it could also be here on earth in a *tzim tzum*. What I do not believe is that it has been destroyed and lost forever. It will show up again either there, here, or everywhere. In other words, the ark of the covenant is made of wood and metal and will pass away when this natural world passes away. But the Spirit that made the ark will be forever and that same Spirit dwells within us and is present wherever the Spirit of God is present, which is everywhere.

I believe in the Trinity. I cannot explain it, but I still hold it as truth. The Jews would call this a *choq*, which is something that you cannot explain, but you believe it because God teaches it and commands you to believe it. This is the same with *tzim tzum*. It is beyond our ability to understand and seems like a contradiction. Just as we do not call the Trinity a contradiction but a paradox, *tzim tzum* is also not a contradiction but a paradox. A paradox is defined as "a statement that is seemingly contradictory or opposed to common sense and yet is perhaps true, a self-contradictory statement that at first seems true, or an argument that apparently derives self-contradictory conclusions by valid deduction from acceptable premises."[4] If we say the Trinity is three Gods in one God, that is a contradiction. However, if we say the Trinity is three persons in one God, that is not a contradiction but a paradox.

This is where I begin to understand what was taking place during the transfiguration. To say that the transfiguration took place in heaven and earth at the same time is a contradiction. To say that Moses and Elijah, who were in heaven, existed with Peter, James, and John in some sort of divine bubble created by Jesus—bringing together the physical and spiritual realms—is a paradox.

What was the purpose of the transfiguration? Why was it necessary for Peter, James, and John to see Jesus conversing with Moses and Elijah? In the Likkutei Sichot Volume XI, pages 8–13, which are a collection of writings by rabbinical sources, we learn that there is an "inter connection between Moses and the Messiah: The Messiah will be brought by the powers transmitted through the former. And hence also their difference: The exile to and liberation from Egypt was for the sake of Giving of the Torah (Exodus

---

4. "Paradox." *Merriam-Webster.com Dictionary*, Merriam-Webster, https://www.merriam-webster.com/dictionary/paradox. Accessed 25 Nov. 2024.

3:13) and this was to give Israel the power to purify themselves and the world. The task of the Messiah is to complete this process, and to innovate the subsequent service, when the purity of the world is complete."[5]

In the Tanya (another rabbinical work) Part IV, 4 we learn: "Just as the Torah (through the hand of Moses) gives the world the power to bring the Messiah, so it gives each and every individual the power to refine his own life and environment, and so hasten the Messianic Age."[6]

We further learn in Genesis 49:10, "*The sceptre shall not depart from Judah, nor a lawgiver from between his feet, until Shiloh come; and unto him shall the gathering of the people be.*" According to the Tanya Part 1 at the beginning of chapter 43, "This is taken to refer to the Messiah, because the words *yavo Shiloh* and *Mashiach* (Shiloh come and Messiah) are numerically equivalent. The same equivalence also applies to the words Shiloh and Moses **so that the coming of the Messiah is related to Moses.** In addition, *yavo* (come) has the same numerical value as *echad* (one). Thus, we can state the equivalence: Messiah = Moses + One, and its meaning is that the Messiah will be brought by service which has the attribute of Oneness; and the power to achieve this is transmitted through Moses."[7]

I have found that throughout Jewish teachings and literature, "the coming of the Messiah is related to Moses." It is also taught that Elijah will herald the coming of the Messiah. We believe this to be John the Baptist, which I agree is a forerunner of the Messiah, but the Jews believe that Elijah will come to not only announce the Messiah but also to denounce false Messiahs.

---

5. Rabbi Menachem Mendel Schneerson, *Likkutei Sichos*, Volume XI. (Kehot Publication Society, 1999), 8–13.

6. Rabbi Schneur Zalman, *Likkutei Amarim – Tanya*, (Kehot Publication Society, 2009), Part IV.

7. Zalman, *Likkutei Amarim – Tanya*, Part I Chapter 43.

In Revelation 11:3 we learn about two witnesses: *"And I will give power unto my two witnesses, and they shall prophesy a thousand two hundred and threescore days, clothed in sackcloth."* These witnesses are not identified, but some say they are Enoch and Elijah, others say they are just two witnesses of that time period. I would suggest that these two witnesses are really Moses and Elijah who come to earth. My personal theory is that they dwell in a *tzim tzum* in a heavenly noncorrupt body like that in which they appeared with Jesus on the Mount of Transfiguration. However, they come to earth in a body like Jesus had after He rose from the dead. So long as they stay in that *tzim tzum*, no one can harm them. But then God permits them to leave the *tzim tzum* and their bodies die only to be resurrected.

The idea is that a heavenly body cannot exist in our earthly realm without leaving the heavenly realm and an earthly, corruptible, sinful body cannot exist in a heavenly realm. Jesus is the only one who could exist both in the physical realm in a corruptible body, a body that is made up of blood cells, skin, and organs that can decay and die, and also exist in a heavenly realm. Jesus was able to move in and out of the *tzim tzum* without the physical body dying.

We will also explore what happens when a physical body is not inhabited with a divine spirit as it was with Jesus. In theology, we talk about the paradox of the incarnation of Jesus. How is it possible to be both God and man at the same time? This is also not a contradiction but a paradox, one of the great paradoxes of Christianity.

In Hebrews 2:7 we learn that Jesus made Himself a little lower than the angels. We also learn in Philippians 2:7–11 that Jesus emptied Himself. This is a simple way to explain or picture *tzim tzum*. *Tzim tzum* are Hebrew words not found in the Bible but are found in extra-biblical literature in Classical Hebrew. In extra-biblical literature, we find teachings of the *'or ein sof* or infinite light,

130 *What the Rabbis Know That I Never Learned in Church*

which had to be reduced or constricted in order for God to create the universe—that is, He had to establish a *tzim tzum* in order to create the physical universe. The physical universe is like a dark bubble in the center of the *'or ein sof*. Light may just be used as a metaphor rather than a reference to a luminary. We do not really understand light itself; we just know it is energy that gives off wave patterns. When Jesus said He is the Light of the World (see John 8:12), He did not necessarily mean He was a glowing object but that He is the essence of all that exists in life. He is the gateway, the doorway between the physical and supernatural realms.

God said, *"See, I have set before thee this day life and good, and death and evil"* (Deuteronomy 30:15). Jewish teachers will point to this verse to demonstrate *tzim tzum*. God had to step aside to create the physical world, but if He were not in it, it would not be good or in harmony with Him but would be entirely evil.

This may be a reason for the flood. *"Noah found grace in the eyes of the LORD"* (Genesis 6:8). Note carefully that Noah *found* grace in the eyes of the Lord. Now I am not going to go all Calvin with you, but I believe the old theologian was on to something with his election theory. Before the flood God withdrew His *tzim tzum* and left humankind to search for Him. The problem was that when God withdrew His *tzim tzum*, all that was left was evil, and because of that humankind did not seek God. So, God had to offer a special grace to Noah to seek Him and thus Noah found this grace. After the flood, this efficacious grace or special grace became part of the nature of humanity, so it would be passed on to each following generation like the sin nature was. Before the flood humankind had no restraint, that is, no conscious saying, "you must choose what is right." Having the knowledge of right and wrong, without the special grace of God, humankind just chose what was wrong.

We now have the ability to distinguish right from wrong, but many confuse them. People often call good things evil and evil things good. So, we are right back to what it was before the flood with humankind choosing evil even though God has given us the ability to choose what is good or in harmony with Him.

> *But as the days of Noah were, so shall also the coming of the Son of man be.* (Matthew 24:37)

What does this have to do with the transfiguration? Peter, James, and John on the Mount with the resurrected Jesus were caught in this bubble of *tzim tzum*. Also, in that *tzim tzum* bubble were the two individuals who the Jews believed would announce and confirm the identity of the Messiah: Moses, and Elijah. Peter, James, and John, three Jewish individuals who would bring the message of Jesus Christ as the true Messiah to the world, witnessed the testimony of these two individuals who were to confirm the identity of the Messiah.

16

SHORTEN THE WAY— KEFITZAT HADERECH

"And when they were come up out of the water, the Spirit of the Lord caught away Philip, that the eunuch saw him no more: and he went on his way rejoicing."
—Acts 8:39

"I was in the Spirit on the Lord's day, and heard behind me a great voice, as of a trumpet."
—Revelation 1:10

"And I knew such a man, (whether in the body, or out of the body, I cannot tell: God knoweth;) How that he was caught up into paradise, and heard unspeakable words, which it is not lawful for a man to utter."
—2 Corinthians 12:3–4

"And unless those days were shortened, no flesh would be saved; but for the elect's sake those days will be shortened."
—Matthew 24:22 (NKJV)

134 What the Rabbis Know That I Never Learned in Church

> *"And I came this day unto the well."*
> —Genesis 24:42

> *"He put forth the form of a hand, and took me by a lock
> of mine head; and the spirit lifted me up between the earth
> and the heaven, and brought me in the visions of God to
> Jerusalem, to the door of the inner gate that looketh toward
> the north; where was the seat of the image of jealousy,
> which provoketh to jealousy."*
> —Ezekiel 8:3

Orthodox Jews have a teaching known as *kefitzat haderech*, the translated meaning as a "shortening of the way." These words themselves are not found in the Bible, but there are ancient sages and rabbis who do believe it is mentioned in the Bible. Genesis 24:42 says, "*And I came this day unto the well, and said, O Lord God of my master Abraham, if now thou do prosper my way which I go.*" Rashi teaches that the usage of "*I came this day*" indicates that, "Today I started my journey and today I have arrived here. Hence we may infer that the earth (the road) shrunk for him (i.e., that the journey was shortened in a miraculous manner.)"[8] Many sages and Jewish teachers point to the grammatical context of Genesis 24:42 to show that this servant completed his journey of four hundred miles in one day, which was impossible unless he had the gift *of kefitzat haderech.*

In fact, Enoch, Elijah, Samuel, Ezekiel, Phillip, and Jesus all demonstrated *kefitzat haderech* as indicated in the above verses. They were all caught away and transported through time and space. In Matthew 24:22 it appears that what is being described is also an occurrence of *kefitzat haderech* in a different manner. Jesus

---

8. "Rashi on Genesis 24:42," Sefaria, accessed December 2, 2024, https://www.sefaria.org/Rashi_on_Genesis.24.42.1?lang=bi.

Shorten the Way—Kefitzat Haderech   135

implies the possibility that for the elect's sake the days could be shortened. Could Jesus have been speaking about *kefitzat haderech* as a gift available for saints living in the last days as a means of protection and evangelization?

There are orthodox rabbis today who believe that God still gives the gift of *kefitzat haderech*. Shmuel Yosef Aganon, an Israeli Nobel Prize winner for literature in 1966, wrote about a righteous rabbi who was given the gift of *kefitzat haderech*, or the ability to transport himself from one place to another. He would transport himself into the treasury of the Habsburg Empire and help himself to some gold coins and then transport himself out before anyone could see him. He had to use the coins to help the poor. If he ever kept any for himself, if he ever used his gift for self-gain, even to receive praise and feed his pride, he would lose the gift of *kefitzat haderech*.

What fascinates me more than anything about this is that the concept of *kefitzat haderech* transcends time. God does not live in time. God created time. Time for us will one day cease. We cannot, in our human state, grasp the idea of no beginning or no ending, yet the very existence of the universe proves the idea of no beginning or ending.

God is living in a constant state of *kefitzat haderech*. It is through *kefitzat haderech* that He can be omnipresent and spend every moment, 24/7, with you personally.

We are told we entertain angels unaware (see Hebrews 13:2). Is it possible these are not all supernatural beings? Could they be flesh-and-blood believers who move through time and space in an instant, encased in a *tzim tzum* bubble that contains both the natural and supernatural realms? They then serve as "messengers" of God to be in a certain place at a certain time to help us along. Like the righteous rabbi in Shmuel Yoesf Aganon's story, if they use the gift for self-gain or pride, they will lose it. Hence, they could never reveal their gift of *kefitzat haderech*, so we would then never learn they had such a gift.

I am not claiming *kefitzat haderech*, but many years ago, when I was working on my doctoral dissertation, I was working part-time in a mailroom. I was thinking about Joseph and how he stored away seven years of grain. I was wondering what these storehouses looked like. Suddenly, I felt like I was in a desert; I could feel the heat and smell the smells. I was looking at a crowd of people. I noticed a chariot ride up surrounded by guards. Then I looked out and saw all these mounds. Suddenly I was back in the mailroom. I was sleep deprived due to my studies; I was very pre-occupied thinking about my research. I realized that I had finally reached my breaking point and needed to get some sleep.

What I wonder about to this day is that my co-worker in the cube next to me said, "Tell me next time you leave to go to the bathroom." I said I did not leave my station, but he insisted I was gone for at least three minutes. Still, I figured I was so deeply in thought that maybe I did in some dream state go the bathroom and saw it as a trip to the Middle East. I am sure there are many natural explanations, not the least an overworked graduate student stressing out over his doctoral dissertation. But that following week as I was doing my research I found an old book by an archaeologist who had drawn pictures of the storehouses in Egypt about the time of Joseph. They looked exactly like what I saw when I was in my semi-trance state. Again, maybe I saw this picture years ago and it was in my subconscious. Or maybe I experienced *kefitzat haderech*. I will never know in this natural realm, but one day I will.

I recall a friend who was an evangelist. He had a revival meeting in a town that was a four-hour drive. He was ministering to someone and lost track of his time and found he only had three hours to make the four-hour trip to the meeting. He called his host and said he was leaving but would be late for the preliminaries; however, he felt he would be on time to deliver the message.

Somehow, he made the four hour trip in three hours and arrived even before the preliminaries. Could this have been an example of *kefitzat haderech?*

17

THE SHECHINAH

"Let them make me a sanctuary;
that I may dwell among them."
—Exodus 25:8

"Behold, Boaz came from Bethlehem,
and said unto the reapers, The Lord *be with you.*
And they answered him, The Lord *bless thee."*
—Ruth 2:4

"Moses was not able to enter the tabernacle of meeting,
because the cloud rested [shakhan] *above it, and the glory of*
the Lord *filled the tabernacle."*
—Exodus 40:35 NKJV

Moses could not enter the Tent of Meeting because of the Shechinah (alternately spelled Shekinah) glory. The Talmud and other Jewish literature are filled with references to the Shechinah glory. Christians despise the word "mystical" and yet the word *Shechinah* that Christians love to use is a mystical word. It is simply referring to the presence of God. The word Shechinah itself is not found in the biblical text. This word is really an extra-biblical word that mystical rabbis coined. They took the word *shakhan*, which literally means a dwelling place, and put it into a Hiphal form, so it literally means "he is caused to dwell." Then they gave it a feminine ending. In Mishnaic Hebrew, the word is often referred to as birds nesting (Talmud Baba Kammah 92b).

Shakhan also means royalty or royal residence. The Greek word *skene* (dwelling) is thought to be derived from *shakhan*. The word "tabernacle" is *mishkan*, which is a derivative of the same root, and it is also used in the sense of a dwelling place. In classic Jewish thought, the Shechinah refers to a dwelling or settling in a special place so that while in proximity to the Shechinah, the connection to God is more readily perceivable. The word *shakhan* is different from *yashav*, which is another Hebrew word that is used for dwelling but has the idea of a permanent residence. *Shakhan* differs in that it means to take up residence in one place for an extended period of time but not with the intention of making it a permanent residence.

When Moses descended Mt. Sinai after being with God, his face shone with the brightness of God such that He had to wear a veil.

> *When Aaron and all the children of Israel saw Moses, behold, the skin of his face shone; and they were afraid to come nigh him.* (Exodus 34:30)

Our bodies are the temple of God (see 1 Corinthians 6:19–20), so the Shechinah glory can also rest in us. Eventually, that glory faded from Moses's earthly body—it was not permanent.

In the story of Ruth we have another example of the Shechinah glory that is manifested just from someone's very presence. Why was Ruth, a Moabite woman, suddenly allowed to marry a Hebrew man? This was allowed as she was a convert to the Jewish faith. Now it is not unusual for someone to convert to Judaism in order to marry someone who is Jewish, which you could accuse Ruth of doing except for an incident recorded in Ruth 2:4. *"Behold, Boaz came from Bethlehem, and said unto the reapers, The Lord be with you. And they answered him, The Lord bless thee."* The word "be" is not in the original Hebrew text. The translator is paraphrasing, assuming this was some sort of greeting. Literally this reads: "The Lord with you." In English, we need a verb to complete a sentence, but in Hebrew you can have a sentence without a verb. I have learned from rabbis that the verb should be "is" not "be." In other words,. "The Lord *is* with you" That is to say: "The Lord is here." The reapers responded, "The Lord *will* bless thee." The word "bless" is in a Piel imperfect form. That means God will surely bless you abundantly. This was not a typical greeting. There was something behind this. When Boaz entered the field, he felt the presence of God as did the reapers who also felt the presence of God and responded. "Yeah, we feel it too. You are really going to be blessed." Then right away he noticed Ruth and asked about her. Not necessarily because of her beauty, but rather because Boaz discerned she was the source of the presence of God that they felt. A foreign woman, a Moabite for crying out loud, glowing with the presence of God or the Shechinah. A little investigation proved she shunned a life of royalty and idolatry to become a proselyte to the Hebrew faith. Ruth said to Naomi, *"Where you live, I will live. Your people will be my people, and your God will be my God"* (Ruth 1:16 NCV).

In Jewish literature the Shechinah is seen to manifest itself most prevalently in the temple and tabernacle. However, the Talmud reports that it may be found in acts of public prayer. "Where ten are gathered for prayer, there the *Shechinah* rest" (Talmud Sanhedrin 39a). It is also found in righteous judgment:

"When three sit as judges, the *Shechinah* is with them" (Talmud Berachot 6a). Jesus quoted from Jewish oral tradition which was later recorded in the Talmud, *"Where two or three are gathered together in my name, there am I in the midst of them"* (Matthew 18:20). I am sometimes criticized for quoting from the Talmud, but Jesus Himself quoted from the Talmud, which was oral tradition during His time on earth. We often think Jesus is referring to prayer in this verse, yet in Jewish tradition they recognize He was making a reference to righteous judgment. The word Shechinah is also found when in personal need. Talmud Shabbat 12b says, "It was also manifested when the prophets prophesied."

> *But now bring me a musician. Then it happened, when the musician played, that the hand of the LORD came upon him* [Elisha].
> (2 Kings 3:15 NKJV)

Elisha then received his prophecy.

Yet, is not God omnipresent? How can He dwell in one location? This is where we really need to understand rabbinic teaching if we are to understand our own theology. The rabbinic teaching is that the omnipresence of God is heavenly and it is His masculine nature, the part that protects, provides, and watches over us. The Shechinah is the earthly, feminine nature that nurtures, comforts, and shares intimately with us. David and the prophets always had the presence of God dwelling within them to protect and provide for them, but it was at the temple or tabernacle where they found that nurturing and caring presence of God, the Shechinah.

Josephus gives an account of Herod raiding the tomb of David and Solomon to acquire the wealth to finance the rebuilding of the temple in Antiquities 14.7.1. Josephus records that as two guards entered the tomb, they were slain by a flame of the Shechinah glory. It shook Herod up so much that he sealed off the tomb, never to re-enter.

The Shechinah 143

Eusebius, church historian and scholar 260-340 CE, records that the Shechinah glory was seen leaving the temple in 66 AD and alighting on the Mount of Olives. Josephus and a witness named Rabbi Jonathan also record the same account. That is why the Mount of Olives is such a special place for Christians. Yet do we need to travel to the Mount of Olives to experience the Shechinah glory?

John said, *"In the beginning was the Word* [logos], *and the Word was with God, and the Word was God....All things were made by him; and without him was not any thing made that was made"* (John 1:1, 3).

The King James Version of 1611, and all versions that have stemmed from it, have attached the masculine gender to the Greek concept of the Logos. Yet, the eight prior English translations give logos a neutral gender: *"By it all things were made."* This is important—look closely. Jesus is the Logos, which is why later translations give it a masculine gender. However, Jewish teaching tells us that it was the Shechinah glory that created the world. Prior to His appearance on Earth, Jesus was the Shechinah glory, and when the physical manifestation ascended to heaven His earthly manifestation as the Shechinah glory remained. Paul tells us that He will never leave us. (See Hebrews 13:5.) The word "leave" in Greek is *aniemi*, which means to tightly embrace. He will never stop embracing us. He cannot do that from heaven. So, although His physical body ascended to heaven, His earthly presence, the Shechinah glory, the feminine nature of nurturing, comforting, remains to *aniemi*, tightly embrace us.

But soft, remember the Shechinah means a dwelling place. Paul makes it clear that this is our earthly bodies: *"We have this treasure from God, but we are like clay jars that hold the treasure"* (2 Corinthians 4:7 NCV). The Shechinah glory now dwells within us.

Yet there is more, the Shechinah glory also demands a physical location. As Jesus went to the garden and Paul to the desert, we too need a place to go. A place where no one else is around and His Shechinah glory can manifest itself to soothe our troubled souls. We need a place, like Jesus found in the garden of Gethsemane, where we can have a time of intimacy with Him. A husband and wife have their little private place that they can go to, where no one else is around and it is there that they can be intimate. Without it the relationship will die. So too we need that private place to go to every day—a garden, a special room, a warehouse—where the Shechinah can manifest itself and we can share an intimacy with our Creator so that relationship will never die and in that place we find that *shakhan* where the Shechinah can *aniemi* or tightly embrace us.

Years ago as I was going through a difficult time in my life, I was offered the opportunity to have access to a warehouse during the night if I agreed to clean the office area. I was allowed to roam that warehouse all night long, praying and seeking the face of God. There was one spot in that warehouse, near the loading docks. I don't know why but when I stepped into that certain spot, I was filled with the presence of God. As I moved away from the spot, the presence lifted, but when I stepped back into it, there it was again. His presence was so nurturing, comforting, and peaceful. Maybe my mind was playing some sort of game, but I am convinced this was the Shechinah being manifested. Throughout my life I have discovered specific areas or spots that I would go to where I could really feel God's presence or His Shechinah. Although God dwells within me as He does with all believers, He does enjoy sharing a special manifestation of His presence in a special location where you and He can be alone together undisturbed.

18

PARDES—
A RABBINICAL BIBLE STUDY METHOD

Pardes is an Aramaic word meaning an orchard or paradise. "Paradise" is the Jewish word for heaven. If you remember the malefactor on the cross who asked Jesus to remember him, Jesus's reply was, *"Today you will be with me in paradise"* (Luke 23:43 NLT).

The word *pardes* or as it is sometimes rendered PaRDeS is also an acronym for a Jewish approach to biblical exegesis used in midrashing. Midrash is a Hebrew word derived from the root word *daresh,* which means to seek out with care, to closely investigate. Exegesis is an in-depth study or interpretation of a biblical text.

PaRDeS represents four levels of study: *Pashat, Remez, Deresh, and Sod.*

PASHAT

Pashat means surface or straight. It is the literal or direct meaning of a passage of Scripture. Most Christians never go beyond that point.

146 *What the Rabbis Know That I Never Learned in Church*

Stop and consider, however: everything God wants us to know about Him and His creation is found in a skinny little book we call the Bible. The God and Creator of the universe gives us all the information about Himself in a short book. As the God of the universe, He could fill an entire library. Surely, He is holding back on us. There must be more to the Creator of the universe than what is found in that book. Well, there is. God said, *"And ye shall seek me, and find me, when ye shall search for me with all your heart. And I will be found of you, saith the* LORD*"* (Jeremiah 29:13–14).

God has given us everything we need to know about Him and about living on this earth in the Bible. It is just that we will not find it all from a surface or literal reading. That would be like looking at the ocean, admiring its waves, vastness, beauty, and many colors but only seeing its surface. So too, with our reading of God's Word, we only see the surface. Most Christians struggle to read the Bible, some have never read it completely, and others read it only when passages are flashed on an overhead screen while a preacher is preaching.

Every year, pastors hand out little pamphlets that divide the entire Bible into 365 daily portions. If you read a portion every day, you will have read through the whole Bible in a year. That is considered such an accomplishment they even have a party at the end of the year to celebrate those who read through the whole Bible. I mean, those are real bragging rights. Many, however, do not make it. Let's face it: a few are chosen for this great task of reading through the Bible in one year, and within every group, there are those who will rise to the top and read every word.

I have a woman who rides my disability bus to the library who says she is a Christian. She takes out a stack of books, novels, mysteries, and romances. Some of these books are longer than the Bible. In about two weeks, I take her back to the library where she exchanges these books for more. She commented one day that she had this plan from her pastor to read through the Bible in one year and was quite proud of the fact that she was on track to finish reading the Bible by the end of the year. Yet, she can read through an Agatha Christie novel in two evenings.

I had a roommate in Bible college whose fiancée back home would write to him every day. One day he received a ten page letter from her. Now he didn't have to divide the letter into ten parts to read a portion a day to read through the whole letter. He read through all ten pages, during our theology class of all things. By the next day he had all ten pages memorized.

Why is it my roommate could read through a ten-page love letter from his fiancée during a theology class and have it memorized within a day or two, yet if some of us were given an assignment to read through ten pages of the Bible, God's love letter to us, we wouldn't finish it? We often make countless excuses to avoid what seems like an impossible task. The difference is that my roommate was in love with the author of that letter. Are we really in love with the Author of the Bible?

The sad fact is that American Christianity is filled with biblical illiterates. At best Christians read the Bible just get the surface understanding. Some will study the Bible, look up passages in a commentary, and might even look up a word in *Strong's Exhaustive Concordance of the Bible* to check out the meaning in Greek or Hebrew. That is studying the Bible, but it is akin to checking out the shallows of the ocean with a snorkel. Then you have some who will put on a scuba tank and diving suit, or enter a research submarine and explore the depths of the ocean. That is accomplished by meditating on the Word of God. We should strive to meditate like David did: *"But his delight is in the law of the LORD; and in his law doth he meditate day and night"* (Psalm 1:2). Pardes is not reading the Bible or even studying the Word of God. It is reading, studying, and meditating on the Word of God. Looking out at the vastness and beauty of the surface of the ocean is the first level of study of Pardes, the *pashat*.

REMEZ

The next step in Pardes, is the *remez*, which means a hint. You catch a glimpse of beauty unseen on the surface, like snorkeling off the shore of the ocean. It is beautiful but only hints to some greater beauty and wonder at an even further depth.

DERESH

So, you move to the next level, *deresh,* and put on a diving suit or enter a research submarine and begin to explore the depths of the ocean that few venture into.

SOD

Finally, you will enter into *sod,* that last level of exegetical study. This is where you not only see the depth of beauty of the Word of God but you experience it as well. This is taking samples from the ocean floor and putting them under a microscope. For you the word *sod* means secret. It is the realm of Bible study and interpretation that only the Holy Spirit can reveal to you. It is God revealing His secrets to you.

Let's apply Pardes to a passage of Scripture. Now normally, you would do this with a study partner or with a group in a Bible study. This involves participation from each member or student as each person is encouraged to listen to the voice of the Holy Spirit and share what they believe the Holy Spirit is sharing with them. The Talmud teaches that one is to never study the Torah alone. We are to search for a study partner to challenge our conclusions. We need to seek the insight of others to get a different perspective to allow for the diversity of experience and relationship with God. God is, after all, a personal God, so let Him be a personal God and share with each other in a personal way.

Psalm 16:11 says, *"You will show me the path of life; In Your presence is fullness of joy; At Your right hand are pleasures forevermore"*

(NKJV). I find that studying a particular Scripture may very well address a personal need. Let's say I had a difficult day driving my disability bus. Most people are grateful and gracious for the ride. Our community provides this door-to-door service for free. We work very hard to meet the needs of our riders. However, on occasion, we get those who feel entitled and consider us their own personal chauffeur. They know the time of their pick-up but wait until the driver beeps the horn to do their last-minute things. Meanwhile I'm running a tight schedule and traffic is building up behind me with impatient drivers honking their horns because they cannot get around my bus. On such days, I find that I start to get into a very unchristian mood.

In the midst of my grumblings, feeling sorry for myself, and trying to find a way for cars to get around me without having to go around the block, I then got a call from my dispatcher asking me to make a special trip for someone they accidentally overlooked. This happened one day, and I did not realize how special that little trip would be.

I had dropped off my last passenger and went to pick up my special trip. I had my worship music playing on my iPod when I pulled in front of her house. Out came an elderly woman who appeared to be approximately ninety years of age. There was something special about her; I could sense she had a sweet spirit. She seemed to radiate a glow, a sort of light. There was a quiet joy and peace that surrounded her. After helping her onto my bus, I moved to the driver's seat and glanced into my review mirror and saw that she was crying. I asked what was wrong and she said, "Oh, nothing, but we sang that song in church last Sunday, and it is so beautiful." She paused a moment and continued, "No, it is not the song that brings the tears; it's the Holy Spirit." The song was titled, "In Your Presence," by the Brooklyn Tabernacle Choir.

I began to listen to the song, and in the words of Maynard G. Krebs it was, "like everything was getting misty." A cloud of glory

150 *What the Rabbis Know That I Never Learned in Church*

seemed to descend upon our bus, and for the first time that day, I felt relaxed and joyful, smiling as I entered into that "*fullness of joy.*"

That is the *pashat*, the surface understanding of "*the fullness of joy.*" But I realized there was something more here, and I could not wait to open my Hebrew Bible and examine the words "*fullness of joy,*" which I did at my next break. My personal experience was my *remez*, the hint that there was a deeper understanding to this fullness of joy. I had experienced something much deeper than just a "*fullness of joy.*" This was something very special, and I had to know more about it.

So now I was ready to enter the third level, the *deresh*, the search for the deeper understanding. I began by looking at the Hebrew words for *fullness of joy*. In Hebrew it is *soba semachot*. The word *semachot* comes from the root word *semchah*, which means joy and serenity. But this word is found in the feminine plural form. How can you have joy in a plural form? It could indicate, as it does in English, more than one. The plural form in Hebrew could also indicate one of two things or even both. Well, there is more than one type of joy in our earthly realm. We find joy in a beautiful sunny day, sharing experiences with a friend, eating a good meal, reading a good book, love, anticipation of a happy event, and so on. We find many different types of joy.

Yet, what the psalmist is saying is that he finds all that joy that we experience in the natural world in just the simple presence of God. The plural in Hebrew could also mean the ultimate, the greatest. The same joy we experience with friends is the same joy we experience with God, only greater. The same joy we experience eating a good meal is the same joy we can experience in consuming the Word of God, only a more intense joy. I found an abundance or fullness of that joy in the presence of God. This expresses the Hebrew plural. Not just a joy but a fullness of joy. Indeed, in that wonderful moment on my bus, I experienced the joy of fellowship with another who also loved Him. I experienced the joy of serenity, peace, and renewed Sabbath energy.

What is this Sabbath energy? It is something I learned from my Jewish friends. Let's dive deeper into the beautiful ocean where we find the word for "fullness" is *soba*, which comes from the same root as Shabbat, which means rest and ceasing from labor. It also has the idea of an abundance and fullness, like a Sabbath rest.

Let's take a closer look into the *deresh* and examine the grammar. The word used as an adjective, *soba*, is in a masculine singular form, yet the noun it modifies is in a feminine plural form. In Hebrew grammar the adjective should parallel the noun it modifies. If the adjective is in a masculine singular form then the noun should be. Ah, another *remez*, a hint in this grammatical anomaly. Plural in Hebrew can mean both more than one and the ultimate or greatest. Hence this joy in the presence of God not only brings all the joys that we can experience in this natural world, but it is also the greatest. Now, this word is a grammatical anomaly as it should be in a masculine form, yet it is in a feminine form. This is specific to the joy of the feminine nature of God, the love, caring, caressing, nurturing, forgiving, and mercy of God. The masculine nature of God is the discipline, provision, and protection. Sure, there is joy in the masculine sense, but the writer created a grammatical anomaly to express the idea that this is a joy that is loving, nurturing, and emotional.

Here on earth, God is a Father, for He protects us, disciplines us, and provides for us. But in heaven, in eternity, we will no longer need the protection, discipline, or provision of a Father; we will have the motherhood of God, the continual loving, nurturing, and motherly caresses of God. The Jews call this the Shechinah which I dealt with in the last chapter.

Another way to look at this is that the Sabbath is like the consummation of a marriage where we as the bride enjoy intimacy with our bridegroom. Hence *soba simchoth* is a joy of being united

152 *What the Rabbis Know That I Never Learned in Church*

as a bride and groom are united as one and enjoy intimacy with each other.

Next, I entered the *sod*, the experience and the application of this depth of reading, study, and meditation. I was miserable before my elderly sister got on the bus. When she got on, she was glowing with the light of God, but I blacked out that light until she said that blessing, "It's not the music. It's the Holy Spirit." She was telling me the Holy Spirit was present during my miserable day. Then I opened my eyes to the Light.

Have you ever attended a Sabbath meal with a Jewish family? You may have noticed on the Sabbath, the mother lights Sabbath candles to introduce the Sabbath. The mother or wife circles the candles three times before she covers her face and says the blessing. I know there are several reasons for this, but I thought of one reason. Orthodox Jews believe that when you enter the Sabbath rest, it is just not sitting back and relaxing. You spend your week exhausting all your energy in work, labors, stress, fears, worries, problems, and so forth. The Sabbath is the day to renew that energy with the Sabbath energy. You notice as the mother or wife circles the candles, she waves her hands over the light of the candles three times. She is inviting the Light of God (Jesus is the Light of God) to enter her, her family, and their souls. I felt that energy of the Light of God enter in fellowship with my elderly sister and then I felt that Sabbath energy enter my soul and then my body.

Perhaps the greatest lesson I could learn from my Jewish friends is that there is much more to the Word of God than just a mere reading. If you love the Word of God like my roommate loved the letters from his fiancée who revealed the secrets of her heart to him, and read it, study it, and meditate on it, God will reveal the secrets or *sod* of His heart to you.

I recall a story about a salesman making a sales call on a florist. As he waited in the office of the florist to attend to a customer, he observed a shelf full of books. One book was a very thick book, the size of an unabridged dictionary. Its title was *Roses*. When the florist returned to his office the salesman asked how someone could write so much about one flower. The florist told the salesman to read the first line of the introduction to the book. It read, "If you love it enough, it will reveal its secrets." So it is that if you love the Lord God and His Word enough, He will reveal His secrets to you.

19

WASHING YOUR HANDS

"Why do thy disciples transgress the tradition of the elders?
for they wash not their hands when they eat bread."
—Matthew 15:2

"Thou shalt not be afraid for the terror by night;
nor for the arrow that flieth by day."
—Psalm 91:5

I have read several commentaries' interpretations of *"the terror by night."* There are many different opinions and schools of thought on this. I will offer my own take on what I believe the psalmist is referring to as *"the terror by the night."*

The word "terror" in Hebrew is the word *pachad*. This carries the idea of a dread or an object of dread. It is something that comes upon you suddenly. The word itself has a built in commentary. The word is spelled *Pei,* which in its shadow form is a reference to being silent out of fear. You are so terrified you cannot even talk. The next letter is the *Cheth*, which in its shadow has the idea of becoming incapacitated by fear. So, the word for terror in its esoteric form suggests a fear so great you cannot speak and you become incapacitated. The final letter is the *Daleth*, which in its positive mode is a doorway to the presence of God, and in its shadow is a doorway or portal to the terrors of hell.

I read on the internet where a special forces officer was sent out with his team on a mission to check out some disturbance that was believed to be a threat to the nation. The internet is the Wild West of the twenty-first century so I am not too sure how much weight to put on this, but it is a good illustration. According to this account, the special forces officer and his team came upon what appeared to be a portal to another dimension. When he looked through that portal, he said what he saw was the terrors of hell itself. He commented that as a special forces officer he had seen the worst possible terrors of mankind, but what he saw through that open portal was far worse than all the terrors he had seen in his life put together. I am not saying the story is true, but I think that is a good example of the word *pachad*. *Pachad* is used to express the terrors of the supernatural world, which would be the world of demonic beings and the Enemy himself.

There is a phenomenon that is very common in children known as night terrors. It is an episode where a child becomes extremely scared and frightened. These episodes could last anywhere from a few minutes up to a half hour. They are sometimes called nightmares on steroids.

The word "night" is *layil* in Hebrew and means the opposite of the day. It is also a word for gloom. As a metaphor, it has the idea of weeping and suffering. The word is also used to express the ideal time to offer pious desires, prayer, praise, and meditation, all with the idea of warding off the forces of evil. Practically all cultures associate the night with a time when evil demonic spirits roam.

They roam at night because that is when our fears can be at their greatest level. It is a time when we are most vulnerable.

Gideon even capitalized on these fears as he attacked the Midianite army at night. As a rule, armies in ancient times did not fight at night. This was not because they could not see who they were fighting; they could easily torch the area to solve that problem. They refused to fight at night because they feared the presence of evil spirits. Even today in the Middle East, many soldiers are so superstitious that they will refuse to fight at night. Just like in the days of Gideon, Israel capitalizes on this because they followed the promise of Psalm 91:5, which tells them that they do not need to fear the terrors of the night and they will carry out covert operations at night.

The Talmud is the written record of oral tradition or what was known in the day of Jesus as the tradition of the fathers. Jesus often challenged the teachings of the traditions of the fathers while also acknowledging some positive aspects of these traditions. In other words, Jesus was not throwing out the baby with the bath water, but He was attacking those areas that violated the Torah or the Holy Scriptures.

A perfect example of this is Matthew 15 where the Pharisees accused Jesus of violating the tradition of the fathers by not instructing His disciples to wash their hands before eating bread. This had nothing to do with good hygiene. The word used for "hands" here is 'aydihun, which means hands but more specifically the fingers and tips of the fingers. The tradition of the fathers, as found in the present-day Talmud, took the Scriptures like Deuteronomy 18:10–12, which declared that consulting familiar spirits, necromancy, enchanting, and witchcraft were an abomination to God, and the tradition of the fathers twisted these words around to make it actually permissible as found in Sanhedrin 65a-b. They cited the very scriptural passage and reversed it, presenting the idea that it was okay to call up demons or spirits to come to your

158 *What the Rabbis Know That I Never Learned in Church*

aid with sorcery as this is not idolatry since the demons were not being worshipped. Yeah, I know, bad Talmud. Apparently, Jesus also agreed this was not good and was, in fact, a violation of the law of Moses. This is what Jesus was blasting the Pharisees about in Matthew 15. The tradition of the fathers and the Talmud teaches that at night the demons will overcome a person when sleeping, and when he awakes the demonic spirit moves into one's hands and the tips of his fingers. It was taught that the demons live in water and love water. You may recall the story of Matthew 8:31–32 where Jesus demanded that demons leave the body of a man and then these demons begged to go into a herd of pigs. When they did, the pigs ran off a cliff into the water. So, the sages taught that you needed to pour water over your hands three times to wash the demons away, especially before eating; you wanted to wash away any remnants of the demons before you pass the demon to your bread and then ingest the demons. I know it sounds crazy, but you have to remember they had no concept of microbes in those days so when a person got sick after eating, they just assumed a demon got into them. Rather than just accept by faith that they were to wash their hands before eating because God had a purpose they could not understand, they tried to make up their own reason for washing their hands and turned it into dogma.

I honestly do not know of any Jews today who buy into this idea of washing demons away even among the most orthodox, but it was really popular among the Pharisees in Jesus's day. The Pharisees explained every ill as something demonic. The tradition of the fathers observed that a person who washed his hands before eating did not come down with an illness, so we can understand how a primitive culture would come to associate the effects of microbes with demons.

This may explain why in verse 24 of the parable of the rich man and Lazarus in Luke 16:19–31, the rich man cried from hell, *"Father Abraham, have mercy on me, and send Lazarus, that he may dip the tip of his finger in water, and cool my tongue; for I am tormented in this flame"* (Luke 16:24). In Aramaic this reads that he was not asking Lazarus to dip the tips of his finger but *tzab'*—that is, wash his finger to moisten his tongue. He said he was in agony. The word "agony" in Aramaic is *mishatanaq*, which is in an Ethpael form, making it reflexive. He is literally causing himself to be in agony in the flame, and it was the demonic forces that were fanning that flame. The word "flame" in Aramaic is *lahav*, which is singular with an indefinite article—that is, a flame. Why not flames? This is a single flame. It is in an emphatic form and would therefore more correctly be used in a metaphoric sense. Fire was often an expression of one's passions. My guess is that demonic forces were causing him to cry out for fulfillment of his physical passions, such as gluttony, alcoholism, and others that would have no fulfillment in his spiritual state. As a spirit, he would have no tongue. The word for "tongue" in Aramaic is *lasan*, which means evil speech. The demonic forces were constantly reminding the rich man of his physical passions. Most likely he would be referencing the evil words formulating in his consciousness that were feeding his physical appetites. Alone in hell, all he could do was meditate on his physical passions, and the demons were making the rich man torment himself with his own physical passions that he lived for while in a physical body. Thus, he was asking Lazarus to moisten his finger because he believed the ancient teaching that the demonic forces were believed to desire water more than tormenting a human being. This may explain why the rich man felt that this moisture from the tip of Lazarus's finger would cause the demonic forces to flee from tormenting him with his passionate physical desires.

In Matthew 15, Jesus is rebuking the Pharisees for twisting the commandments of God around to the point where they were breaking the commandments and then accusing Jesus of breaking the tradition of the fathers that was violating the commandments.

And you thought some of our fringe religious teachings today are crazy? Jesus really had His hands full.

This brings us to the terrors of the night. I believe it is a reference to demonic activity, or the fear of demonic activity and the promise of this psalm is that we don't need to fear even the demons of hell if we are safely wrapped in the shadow of His wings. We are safely covered by the blood of Jesus and we have no reason to fear any demonic activity.

My brother and sister-in-law were Bible translators in a little village in Papua New Guinea. One night, as they prepared for bed in their grass hut, my brother looked out of the window and saw a man sitting in a tree watching them. My brother stuck his head out of the window and shouted, "What are you doing? You're not supposed to do that—watch us as we prepare for bed. Now go on, get out of here." The man instantly jumped from the tree and ran as if he were running for his life.

The next morning my brother called all the villagers together and addressed the chief, "Who was that man in the tree? You must tell your people they don't sit in trees and watch people get ready for bed."

The chief's eyes grew very large, and he looked back at his people, who were just as wide-eyed. The chief asked: "Andy, you saw him?"

"Of course I saw him," replied my brother.

"What did you do?" asked the chief. My brother said he told the man to leave.

There was a gasp from the people and the chief hesitantly asked, "What did he do?"

My brother said, "Well, he took off running."

When my brother said that, suddenly all the people moved away from him, whispering to each other. From that time on, they appeared to be afraid of my brother and showed him almost patronizing respect, which was very disconcerting for my brother, who needed a more informal relationship with the people to carry on his work.

A few days later, my brother traveled to a neighboring village where the people and chief were Christians. The chief was helping my brother out as a sort of consultant in his translation work. My brother told the chief this story, and the chief's eyes took on the look of shock and concern, and he asked, "Andy, you mean you actually saw him?"

My brother said, "Of course."

The chief moved a little closer to my brother and asked, "You actually told him to leave and what did he do?"

My brother said, "He took off running as if someone was chasing him."

When my brother said that, the chief clapped his hands, put them in the air, and began to praise the Lord.

My brother said, "Ok, what's going on? I mean, I would like to praise the Lord over this too."

The chief explained, "Andy, that man was the shaman, the witch doctor. He was trying to put a curse on you."

My brother said, "Oh."

"Andy," the chief continued, "he has the power to make himself invisible. You were not supposed to see him, but for some reason you did."

My brother said, "Oh."

"Andy," the chief said further, "no one yells at the witch doctor, let alone orders him around, yet you commanded him to leave. No one can make the witch doctor leave, but you did."

My brother said, "Oh."

"Everyone is afraid of the witch doctor, but you had no fear whatsoever." My brother said, "Oh."

So, my brother went back to the Amanab people and gathered the villagers around him and told them that it was not he who was able to see the witch doctor and command him to leave, but it was the Spirit of God who lives inside of him.

The point of this story is that if this terror by night really speaks of demonic activity, Psalm 91:5 is telling us we have nothing to fear. My brother was not even aware of demonic activity or even gave it much thought. He was busy going about his Father's business and his Father just filled him with His Spirit so that if any demon tried to get close to him, all he had to do was say, "Get out of here," and that demon would run away in terror. Not because of my brother but because of the God that dwelled inside of him.

I spent several years working for Dr. Lester Sumrall, who was noted for his deliverance ministry. His books covered many areas of demonology and personal experiences in delivering people all over the world from demonic oppression and possession. When I was offered the opportunity to join his organization, I had a moment of pause. I wanted to be sure I fully understood where this man of God stood on various issues, so I began to read his books. The one thing that convinced me that I wanted to work for this man and be mentored under him was when he said, "You have absolutely nothing to be afraid of from the demonic world." We are taught by so many of the dangers and pitfalls of demonic activity and we are warned to be careful yet Dr. Sumrall, who was an expert in the field, believed with his whole heart 1 John 4:4, *"Ye are of God, little children, and have overcome them: because greater is he that is in you, than he that is in the world."* I knew this was one teacher I wanted to sit under because he not only preached the Bible, but he also believed every word of it and he believed the Bible taught we had nothing to fear when we are safely in the arms of Jesus.

My studies of ancient Jewish thought only showed how ridiculous our fears of the demonic world could be. People in ancient times feared demonic forces so much they sought natural means to ward off demonic activity. Jesus taught that it was clearly through His Spirit that demonic activity will flee from us.

20

YIREDU OUR RELATIONSHIP WITH ANIMALS

"'But among the Israelites not a dog will bark at any person or animal.' Then you will know that the LORD makes a distinction between Egypt and Israel."
—Exodus 11:7 (NIV)

"Then came she and worshipped him, saying, Lord, help me. But he answered and said, It is not meet to take the children's bread, and to cast it to dogs. And she said, Truth, Lord: yet the dogs eat of the crumbs which fall from their masters' table. Then Jesus answered and said unto her, O woman, great is thy faith: be it unto thee even as thou wilt. And her daughter was made whole from that very hour."
—Matthew 15:25-28

"Rabbi Judah said in the name of Rav, 'It is forbidden for a person to eat before feeding his animals' as it is written in Deuteronomy 11:15, 'I will give grass in your fields

for you animals,' and only afterward does the Torah say,
'And you will eat and be sated.'"
—The Talmud Gittin 62a

"Neither shall you eat any meat that is torn by beasts in
the field; you shall throw it to the dogs (Exodus 22:30).
This is to teach us that Gd does not deprive any creature
of its just reward. Because the dogs did not bark at the
Israelites when they came out of Egypt (see Exodus 7:11).
Gd said: Give them their reward."
—Taken from the Shemot Midrash Rabbah

We are always reminded that man's best friend is his dog. As any canine lover knows, the word God spelled backward is dog. In fact, in Hebrew the word dog is *kalav*, which, if you consider the letter *Kap* as a preposition like "and," the root word as *lev* for "heart," you have *kalav*, dog, meaning "like a heart."

In Genesis 1:26 we learn that God gave humans dominion over the animals. In English, the word "dominion" means to have sovereignty or control. In other words, we are to rule over them. But our Christian translators assumed that the word "dominion" comes from the root word *radah*. Jewish scholars argue that the root word is *yired*. There is a big difference, for *yired* has the idea of lowering yourself to show respect and honor. We are to respect God's creation and honor it.

I recently drove a veteran to the veteran's hospital. He was a former Army Ranger who served in the Iraq War and the War in Afghanistan. He was assigned to be a dog handler. He trained his dog Nature to sniff out mines and then took him out to minefields to help his unit clear them. I asked jokingly if the dog was given a military rank. He said, of course, his dog did have a military rank, and he was an E-7, Sergeant First Class, a senior non-commissioned officer. I then asked this veteran what his personal rank was, and he said he was an E-6, Staff Sergeant, which is a junior non-commissioned officer. His dog outranked him; Nature was one grade above him.

I learned that the military always gives a dog a rank at least one grade higher than his handler. As a higher-ranking officer, any mistreatment of the dog will result in severe disciplinary action for the handler, on the same level as if he mistreated any superior human officer, thus ensuring the dog is treated well within the military.

When I was told this, I could not help but think of the passages of Scripture quoted in the beginning of this chapter and the quote from the Talmud that teaches one is to feed his animals before he feeds himself to show respect and honor for them. I often wondered about the story in Matthew 15 where Jesus literally called a desperate mother seeking healing for her daughter a "dog." Then Jesus considered this Gentile woman as having great faith when she said that the dogs eat the crumbs from the table of a Jew.

Well, if you understand Jewish tradition and teaching, you realize that Jesus was impressed with this Gentile woman's knowledge of the Jewish faith and Scripture. Note Jesus told this Gentile woman that it was not *meet* to take the bread of children and give it to dogs. The word "meet" in Hebrew is *shaper*, which is a word used for the placenta. The placenta is a temporary embryonic and later fetal organ that begins developing the cell mass that forms the embryo. The placenta connects the fetus to the umbilical cord. What Jesus was saying is that the Jews are going to give birth to Christianity or the church and that it was not yet time for the Gentiles. But this Gentile woman showed her knowledge of the Jewish faith and oral tradition that taught one should feed his animals before themselves. Just as Sergeant Nature outranked his handler, so too, God allowed this Gentile to outrank the Jews. Jesus came to the Jews first to fulfill the prophecy of a Messiah, and

168 *What the Rabbis Know That I Never Learned in Church*

they were His primary focus, yet He was also committed to ensure that the Gentiles were protected, just as the military affords protection for its animals by giving them a higher rank.

Why were animals honored and respected among the Jews? There are many reasons but for me the key reason is that the animals were created to give us a physical glimpse of the heart of God. This is shown nowhere better than in man's best friend the dog.

Several months ago, my study partner acquired a little puppy. She gave it the name Moxie. I recall when we drove out to the kennel to pick Moxie up. It was an hour-and-a-half drive. On the way back, I drove the car while my study partner held her new little puppy. He peacefully laid in her lap as she gave him occasional hugs and kisses. Eventually, the little beggar became car sick and spilled his cookies, and then relieved himself on my study partner's coat. We had to stop at a gas station while my study partner ran into the rest room to clean up and purchase some paper towels. While she was taking care of cleanup I was left alone in the car with Moxie. Little Moxie, who had been quite calm and peaceful, suddenly became very agitated and tried to escape from my car, and I had to hold him the entire time my study partner was in the little convenience store. As he strained trying to escape my clutches, he began to whimper and stare intently out the window, waiting for my study partner's return. When she did not return right away, he stuck his nose in the air, opened his mouth and began to howl like he was calling for her or throwing a tantrum, I am not sure which. Once she did return, he jumped out of my arms and into hers and began to cover her with kisses as she hugged him and kissed him. The defilements he had recently left were all forgotten, his misdeeds were all forgiven, and Moxie rewarded his new pet mommy's forgiveness with dozens of little kisses.

It was then my spirit was quickened, and I decided that Moxie had taken me on a spiritual journey. This instant bonding between my study partner and Moxie reminded me of the day I gave my life to Jesus. I felt so at peace and at home in the arms of Jesus I just wanted to stay that way forever. Then when I suddenly did not feel his loving embrace, like Moxie, I began to panic and longingly reached out for that embrace again.

On the other hand, I pictured Moxie's bonding and longing for my study partner's hugs and kisses. This is just like God and how He longs for us. The story of the prodigal son teaches us that when the son returned, the father saw him walking down the road and ran to him, fell upon him, and hugged and kissed him. This father had been waiting, watching, and longing for his son's return. We know this because he saw his son when he was walking home. (See Luke 15:11–32.)

I am always amazed when I dog sit for my study partner as she runs some errands and how Moxie struggles and fights to escape from my arms as she walks out the door. As the door closes, he jumps out of my lap and runs for the door. Then he jumps up to the window and watches through it as she gets into her car and drives off. Moxie barks, howls, and whimpers as she drives off. After he calms down, he just lays by the door, waiting for her return.

I can't help but think that this is so like our heavenly Father who longs for our return when we fall away from Him into our passions. He can spend all His time focused on just you and then move through time to focus His entire attention on me. His world revolves around you just as Moxie's world revolves around my study partner. He longingly waits for you, and when you return, He covers you with kisses, jumping up and down out of pure joy at having you in His presence. God has nothing else to do but to sit and wait for you to return to Him. He waits with longing and anticipation, and when you do return, He is filled with joy, ready to hug and kiss you.

The Bible tells us that our God is a jealous God. (See Deuteronomy 4:23–24.) Isn't jealous something bad? It can be if it crosses a certain line. Does Moxie cross that line? There was a point when my study partner had another little dog but had to give him away because Moxie and her other dog, Shiloh, were constantly fighting. If she was petting and showing attention to Shiloh, Moxie immediately ran over and tried to nudge his way into that little love affair as if he was saying, "No, no, she is my mommy, not yours." One day as Moxie tried to force his way into the attention of my study partner, I could not help reminding her that, "Thou shall have no other dog before me." Shiloh started to growl menacingly. Little Moxie backed off, but almost immediately, after the tension died down, Shiloh walked over to Moxie, put his paw on top of him and snuggled up to him as if to say, "I know she is your mommy; I am sorry."

Personally, I find nothing wrong with having a jealous God who demands that we have no other God before Him. I mean, I am quite flattered that God loves me so much that He wants my full devotion, attention, and love, just as Moxie longs for my study partner's full attention and love. After all, just like Moxie, I depend upon God for all my needs and He fulfills those needs. I need the security of His love. He is my world, just as my study partner is Moxie's world.

Recently, I was talking with my study partner on the phone when suddenly, I heard a little yelp. She immediately started saying, "Oh, Moxie, I am so sorry," and then I heard her kissing Moxie and apologizing. Apparently, Old Mox is so little that she occasionally steps on him. When she does, she instantly picks him up and apologizes and tells him how sorry she is, and Moxie simply gives her kisses. He forgives her before she even apologizes. Moxie does not understand the words "I am sorry." What he understands is her sincere heart and her heartbreak over having wounded little Moxie. So, Moxie just kisses her to assure her he is okay.

Sometimes Moxie will get a little too frisky and maybe do some damage. He loves to eat her pens. She just cannot keep a pen around and Moxie will find it and start to chew on it. Puppies do chew, and my study partner gets so frustrated with him that she yells at him. The poor little guy feels so bad that he offended his beloved mommy that he puts his head down and looks up at her with those sad eyes. His little heart is broken. My study partner immediately picks him up, kisses him, and assures him she still loves her little Mox. Moxie rewards her with dozens of little kisses; all is instantly forgiven.

I cannot help but think of how many times I stepped on God's love for me by committing some sin, either intentionally or unintentionally. Sometimes I even get angry with God and sort of tell Him off. Yet, when I go to Him apologizing, I find He has already forgiven me. (See Colossians 2:13.) His only concern is that there might be some rift in our relationship. When I assure Him I have no problems, my misstep was not intentional or just a moment of passion, but I still love Him, He responds with complete forgiveness, as if I had never sinned. He is only joyful that our bond is restored.

The Bible teaches that God is close to the brokenhearted. (See Psalm 34:18.) He is close to the brokenhearted because He understands a broken heart more than anyone. We break His heart every day. Like Moxie, God has an easily broken heart, but He is also ready and anxious to forgive that wounding of His heart and restore our relationship with Him.

You see, the main reason God hates sin is because it creates a rift in our relationship with Him. He longs for a relationship without any hindrances. The enemy wants us to sin because He knows that will separate us from God and create a break in our love with Him, and the enemy hates nothing more than when God and you are sharing an intimate relationship. The enemy hates love.

My study partner stays busy with our ministry, not only doing all the administrative work but also teaching and preparing for her teaching. It keeps her busy, and little Moxie, like any puppy, wants her to play with him, take him for walks, and spend all her time with him, which she really can't do. But whenever she is ready to play, Moxie is right there, ready, willing, and able to play and take his walks.

I can't help but think how little we appreciate a God always ready to give and receive our attention and love. He is never too busy for us, and like the Mox, who will patiently lay at my study partner's feet while she is working on her computer, God is right there by our side, patiently waiting for us to put down our daily tasks to spend a few moments to play and go for a walk with Him. Yes, we must go about our daily tasks and responsibilities; God understands, but when we have a free moment to spend with Him, we will always find Him ready and willing to spend that time with us. Do we realize this? Do we appreciate it?

Do you serve God, or does God serve you? Do you exist for God or for you? Moxie loves Laura, my study partner, with no strings attached, with no conditions. God gave us our furry friends to teach us what unconditional love is like. In our observance of Moxie, Shiloh, or any other loyal pet, we get a glimpse of the love that God has for us.

My study partner never abuses this love, never takes it for granted, and nurtures it, feeds it, and cares for it. As a result, she receives the maximum benefit of that unconditional love. So, too, God loves us, cares for us, and longs for us, but for us to receive the maximum benefit of that love, we must feed it, care for it, and nurture it. Again, I remind you that it may be no coincidence that God spelled backward is dog. Dogs are one of many of His creations to reflect and remind us of His amazing *racham* love.

That little lesson from the rabbi who taught me that the root word for "dominion" is *yiredu* and not *radah*, to show respect and honor to God's created beings rather than dominate over them, has not only increased my appreciation for the animal kingdom but has caused me to learn many spiritual lessons from just observing His creation.

21

THE MESSIAH

"And she shall bring forth a son, and thou shalt call his name
Jesus: for he shall save his people from their sins."
—Matthew 1:21

"For unto you is born this day in the city of David a Saviour,
which is Christ the Lord."
—Luke 2:11

The most common reference to our Savior is the name Jesus. The name given to Him at birth by His mother and father, who spoke a Northern dialect—that is, an Old Galilean dialect of Aramaic— was *Eshoa*. The Hebrew form of this name is *Yeshua*, but it is only a short rendering. It's like calling David, Dave. The full and formal rendering of the name is *Yehoshua*, which means Jehovah will save. It comes from the Semitic root *ysha*, which means to help, rescue, deliver, or to save. Our English form is taken from the shortened form Yeshua, which we pronounce in English as Joshua, when the

174 *What the Rabbis Know That I Never Learned in Church*

Semitic letter Yod becomes a J in Latin and is carried over into English. The Greek form is taken from the shorter rendering of Yeshua and is *Iesour* and the Latin *Iesus* which we get our present rendering of Jesus.

Some Christians reprimand me for not using the Hebrew form Yeshua when I speak of Jesus. How could I, as a Hebrew teacher, not use Jesus's real name? I do use His real name! I just use our English pronunciation, Jesus. Oh, you mean the Hebrew pronunciation? Why? That is not His birth name. The Hebrew is only a Hebrew pronunciation of His birth name, Aramaic *Eshoa*. Why not use pronunciations from other languages? In Spanish the pronunciation is *Hay-soos*, Russian is *Esus*, French is *Izeuz*, and German is *Yezus*. The point is that even those who criticize me for not using what they consider the proper name of Jesus—*Yeshua*—are not even speaking his name correctly in Hebrew. They should say *Yehoshua*, but still, they are not using the correct pronunciation of His birth name, which is the Aramaic form *Eshoa*. As Shakespeare said, "What's in a name? That which we call a rose by any other word would smell as sweet."

Jesus is the name I grew up to cherish. It is the name I called upon to make Him my Savior. It is the name I call upon when in trouble, and the name I use when I tell Him how much I love Him. Any other form of that name has no real emotional meaning for me. A man may kiss his wife and say, "Good morning, Gloria." It just would not have the impact of, "Good morning, my beautiful little rose who just bloomed." A rose by any other name may still smell as sweet, but I will use whatever name my heart speaks out to Him, for He listens to my heart, not what comes out of my mouth.

We find that Jesus is also called a Savior. Well, does not the name Jesus mean a Savior? It indeed does, but the Aramaic in Luke uses the word *paruqa*, which means to divide, disconnect, or forcibly remove. After all, is that not what a savior does? He disconnects by forcibly removing you from a threatening position. Jesus removes us from a sinful position to one in harmony with God. But you can see how the Jews of the first century misunderstood the role that Jesus was to play, and that is to save us from our sins.

The Jews were looking for a Savior from national or governmental oppression. Up to the time of captivity, the Middle East was made up of relatively small kingdoms like Edom, Amon, Judah, and so on. The only vast kingdom was Egypt, which had no genuine desire to conquer these smaller kingdoms, as they had nothing Egypt needed in natural resources, which are the basis of many conflicts. As long as they had a healthy trade, why waste their resources by trying to rule over them? However, in the Mesopotamian regions, water, fertile ground, and other resources were not readily available in any one particular kingdom. Hence there were constant conflicts over water rights and fertile land.

By the eighth century BC, imperial powers like Assyria and Babylon began to seek the resources of other kingdoms to make their kingdom wealthy. The small armies of Israel and its allies could not cope with the vast, powerful armies of these imperial kingdoms. As a result, they cried out for a savior (*paruga*) to arise and defeat these powerful imperial armies. By the time of Jesus, the greatest imperial kingdom in the world was the Roman Empire, which taxed them, ruled over them, and enslaved them.

The name Eshoa was very popular. The Jews had only one name in the first century; rather than a last name, they were identified as the son of someone or from the land they came from. Hence, Jesus was called Jesus of Nazareth as that was the town He came from. Many parents named their sons Eshoa, in the hope that they would rise to be a great military and political leader who would save their people from government oppression. That is why Matthew 1:21 is very specific. His name will be called Jesus or Savior because he will save His people from their sins, not from the Roman Empire.

He is also called Christ the Lord in Luke. The word "Lord" in Aramaic is *mara'*, which means an owner or one who possesses land or property. He is the Christ who owns the world or all that exists. The word "Christ" in Aramaic is *Mashicha* or *Moshiach* in Hebrew. This means the anointed one. In general, the Jews do not believe the Messiah will be an incarnation of God but simply a great leader. However, orthodox Jews like the Chabad believed that the 6th Rebbe of Chabad Lubavitch, Yoseph Yitzchak Schneersohn, was the Messiah. They believed he was the essence and existence of God who had placed Himself in a body. Although he has died, he will one day be resurrected and will return to establish peace on earth—which is what we say about Jesus.

According to the Thirteen Fundamental Principles of the Jewish faith listed by Maimonides, the Messiah will bring the ultimate redemption to the world; he will bring an era of world peace, prosperity, and wisdom as well as the resurrection of the dead. He will be a descendent of David who will usher in the Messianic era by rebuilding the temple, bringing or gathering all the Jewish people from the four corners of the earth, and leading them to the promised land. This is when the world will *"beat their swords into plowshares, and their spears into pruninghooks: nation shall not lift up a sword against nation, neither shall they learn war any more"* (Micah 4:3). Man will be preoccupied with only one pursuit, the study of godly wisdom.

> *They shall not hurt nor destroy in all my holy mountain: for the earth shall be full of the knowledge of the LORD, as the waters cover the sea.* (Isaiah 11:9)

The eventual coming of the Messiah is a strongly upheld belief in Judaism; trying to predict the actual time of his coming is frowned upon, as it is or should be in Christianity with the return of Jesus the Messiah. So, when will the Messiah come? It will be when the world needs His coming the most; i.e., when the world

The Messiah 177

is so sinful and in desperate need of salvation, then the Messiah will come. The Talmud tells the story of a rabbi who encountered a prophet and asked him when the Messiah would return. The prophet said, "Today." The rabbi anxiously awaited all day for the Messiah to come, and when he didn't, he went back to the prophet and asked why he did not come. The prophet said, "Today, if you will but harken to his voice."

We can say the same in our Christian faith with the return of Jesus. Books on the second coming fly off the bookshelves. Preachers and teachers build large platforms sharing their ideas about when Jesus will return. Yet, will I tell you when He will return? *"To day if ye will hear his voice"* (Psalm 95:7). For He is ready to live inside you today and bring you peace and comfort until you see Him face to face. I wonder about Christians so anxious for the second coming, calling it "the blessed hope," when they can enjoy His presence right here and now. I don't need the second coming; I have all of God's presence I need and desire within me right now. Oh, but, you say, our Christian concept of a second coming includes a rapture where we get to go to heaven without dying. Well, let me introduce you to the Jewish idea of a rapture.

22

A JEWISH RAPTURE

*"And there came out a fire from the LORD,
and consumed the two hundred and fifty men that offered
incense. And the LORD spake unto Moses, saying, Speak
unto Eleazar the son of Aaron the priest, that he take up the
censers out of the burning, and scatter thou the fire yonder;
for they are hallowed. ... To be a memorial unto the children
of Israel, that no stranger, which is not of the seed of Aaron,
come near to offer incense before the LORD;
that he be not as Korah, and as his company:
as the LORD said to him by the hand of Moses."*
—Numbers 16:35–37, 40

This is an interesting story when viewed from a Jewish mindset. It revolves around the story of Korach (Korah), who incited a mutiny that challenged Moses's leadership and granted the priesthood to Aaron. Korach, a Levite, is accompanied by Dathan and Abiram from the tribe of Reuben, who join in this coup d'état as well as 250 *nasi* from various other tribes. The *nasi* were leaders of their community, respected and righteous men. This is where this story gets a little tricky.

Korach was a member of the tribe of Levi but not in their direct line of Aaron. He was a member of the Kehatites, the most prestigious of the Levite families. This whole dispute came down to simply a matter of class warfare. Korach wanted to be the high priest, and he promised that if he were to be a high priest, he would make everyone equal. Would he eliminate the elitism of the priesthood?

Here is the simple question: why would 250 members of the elite of Israel rebel against the elitism of the priesthood? There was no real political power in the priesthood. These 250 men had all the political power they could want as leaders of their tribes. The priests were merely servants of God, performing the duties of running and maintaining the tabernacle. They had to live off the goodwill offerings of the other eleven tribes. They owned no land; they engaged in no commerce as merchants or businesspeople. They were not like preachers or evangelists of today, who maintain a certain amount of political power. If we were to make a comparison, it would not be with the hierarchy and prestige of the clergy other than those from the house of Aaron. For the most part, the Levites would hold a position about as enviable as a monk in a monastery, serving as a nun, or even a missionary. No one wants to be a part of that unless they have a burning desire to serve God or to draw close to God. There was no material or fleshly advantage to being a part of the priesthood.

What the rebels did was something good; they showed their desire to be close to God and rebel against the dynastic structure of the priesthood. Korach said it himself: he declared that they desired to be like the priest whose sole job was to serve God and draw close to Him, but they were forced to live ordinary lives.

They united against Moses and Aaron and said, "You have gone too far! The whole community of Israel has been set apart by the LORD, and he is with all of us." (Numbers 16:3 NLT)

This rebellion wasn't about land rights, food, money, or political power. It was all about the advantage the priest had of serving God and drawing close to Him. It was an advantage that they perceived they did not have simply because they were not born into the family of Levi.

They declared that the Lord set apart the whole community, and the Lord was with all of them. So why could a person not serve as a priest if he wanted to have the opportunity to enter the priesthood? Why could a Reubenite or a Benjamite not serve as a priest and carry the holy censors if they wanted?

Now the story gets really interesting, and this is where we can find a present-day application. Although the ground does not crack open and swallow us up, we are guilty of the same thing today. We are not jealous of a position or power structure, but we perceive that someone in the ministry is somehow closer to God than a janitor or waitperson. How many factory or service workers run to their priest, pastor, or prophet to be prayed over if they need a healing or some favor from God rather than run to a godly father, mother, or grandparent? How many would ask their brother or sister to pray over them instead of a godly leader?

Of course, you will choose a pastor or priest over your own mother or father to pray for you because that pastor and priest are closer to God. Oh, and if it is a bishop or ADS (Area Denominational Supervisor) who happens to be available, that is even better yet, for we perceive that the higher up you are in the church, the closer to God you are. You could imagine the results if the pope prayed for you—that is almost like talking to God Himself. God is almost guaranteed to answer prayer if the pope prays for you.

Things have not changed since the days of the Hebrews. We somehow have this idea that a seminary graduate is closer to God than a random person walking down the street. The Hebrews thought similarly that those born into a Levitical family were closer to God. Well, Korach and his 250 radicals knew anyone can be close to God. They demanded their piece of the priestly pie. "If my little Reuben wants to grow up to be a priest and carry the incense, well doggone it, he has the right to go to seminary and learn how to carry the incense. Just because his last name is not Cohen doesn't mean he should be denied that right."

Well, they had a good point, but they were ahead of their time. That revolution wouldn't take place for another thousand years and would be led by the Messiah Jesus Christ.

> *But ye are a chosen generation, a royal priesthood, an holy nation, a peculiar people; that ye should shew forth the praises of him who hath called you out of darkness into his marvellous light.* (1 Peter 2:9)

Today, we have Bible schools and seminaries in practically every town. Anyone's son or daughter can attend, graduate, and be ordained a minister of the gospel. Now, whether or not God called them to that ministry is another matter. Yet, anyone who desires to be a priest unto God can be because we were all made priests by the Messiah Jesus Christ.

The fact is that God is willing to be close to everyone who wanted to be close to Him. They do not have to be a priest. There is nothing more special about a priest in God's eye than a simple farmer—both are precious to Him. He created some as farmers and some as priests; God does not play favorites. We all have a role to play in this world. We all have a mission to accomplish, a purpose for our lives.

The perception that someone who is a priest has special influence on God is a deception from the pits of hell, and that is where the perpetuators of such a deception ended up, literally.

> *Then Moses spoke again to Korah: "Now listen, you Levites! Does it seem insignificant to you that the God of Israel has chosen you from among all the community of Israel to be near him so you can serve in the LORD's Tabernacle and stand before the people to minister to them? Korah, he has already given this special ministry to you and your fellow Levites. Are you now demanding the priesthood as well? The LORD is the one you and your followers are really revolting against! For who is Aaron that you are complaining about him?"*
> (Numbers 14:8–11 NLT)

Moses was telling these 250 followers of Korach that they already had the privilege of drawing close to God, but they still wanted to be priests to stand before the people and perform priestly functions. Now Moses was getting to the heart of the issue and addressing the factors of pride, power, and influence. Is it drawing close to God that you want? Or, is it really just to have that sense of being spiritually superior to others? We assume that the 250 rejected this notion and refused to admit to their pride. But how do we know that for sure? Scripture is not clear if they examined their motives or not. It is possible they still longed to be close to God despite having ulterior motives.

I have met many pastors who were godly men. I could sense the presence and power of God on their lives, yet I could not help but feel that they bore a sense of entitlement because they had reverend before their name. I remember one pastor I knew when I was a young pastor myself who I would go to for counsel. My kid brother who eventually worked for this pastor as his assistant used to say, "When people pray, God listens, but when Pastor A prays, God smiles." Yet, I also sensed pride in him. He was ambitious and eventually drove his church into bankruptcy with his schemes of building a mega church. People literally worshipped this man and would go to him before anyone else to be prayed over, feeling he had some special connection to God, and I never heard him deny such a thing. I honestly believe he felt he had the ear of God more than anyone in his congregation. I believe he truly loved God with all his heart, but he was also human and there was no one who could reel him in when he felt he was commissioned by God.

I believed God was using him despite this human tendency to take himself and his position as a pastor too seriously. Time eventually proved he was following his own plan and not God's. His great plans to build a conference center and Christian college with a television network never left the ground. What little he was able to build went into bankruptcy before they held their first conference. God took him home a year later. Despite his earthly failures, I believe with all my heart he met Jesus with that divine kiss. If I didn't believe that, there would be little hope for me.

I still believe Pastor A was a man of God with prophetic gifts. He was also a human being with human flaws like all of us. Whatever God's plan was for Pastor A it was fulfilled, and Pastor A is home in the heart of the God he dearly loved. The people of Israel did not realize that a special position of priesthood also came with special responsibilities.

Frontline soldiers receive the most fire from the enemy. They need the prayer support of all those who are not on the front lines. These support soldiers spent their time in war repairing airplanes and tanks, shipping goods to the war zones, building bases, working out logistics, and all the other support functions for soldiers on the front lines. They may not have had active combat stories to tell, but they fulfilled their duties, they saluted their flag, and they were prepared to face danger if necessary. They deserve the same honor of anyone who wore the uniform and were honorably discharged when their service ended.

The issue before the 250 was simply they wanted to serve on the front lines; they wanted some of that glory even though they already wore the "uniform" of the chosen of God.

When judgment time came, God showed who His chosen frontline warriors for the specific task of priesthood and spiritual leadership were and who were not. Those who were not ended up sucked under by an earthquake.

> "But if the LORD does something entirely new and the ground opens its mouth and swallows them and all their belongings, and they go down alive into the grave, then you will know that these men have shown contempt for the LORD." He had hardly finished speaking the words when the ground suddenly split open beneath them. The earth opened its mouth and swallowed the men, along with their households and all their followers who were standing with them, and everything they owned. So they went down alive into the grave, along with all their belongings. The earth closed over them, and they all vanished from among the people of Israel. All the people around them fled when they heard their screams. "The earth will swallow us, too!" they cried. Then fire blazed forth from the LORD and burned up the 250 men who were offering incense.
>
> (Numbers 16:30–35 NLT)

The 250 *nasi*, the elite of every tribe, the men of renown, however, were not sucked up by the earthquake. They were consumed by the fire of God. Moses said nothing about the fire of God consuming those who showed contempt for the Lord; only those who were swallowed up by the earth showed contempt for the Lord. Why were the men who offered incense not swallowed up by the earth? Maybe because they did not show contempt for the Lord.

The word contempt is *na'ats* in the Hebrew. It is really a word for rejection. Korach and his followers, who were sucked up by the earthquake, rejected the Lord. The 250 did not reject the Lord;

they rejected the message of Moses that they were already fulfilling the roles they were meant to have. Maybe they really did sincerely want to be close to God and felt that the elitism of the priesthood stood in their way. After all, they came with their incense offering.

Now, that is the crux of this matter—the censors with the incense offerings. This was what the sons of Aaron carried to the holy of holies when they were struck down by fire. It is almost a footnote in verse 35 that the 250 were consumed by fire. Like Aaron's sons, they wanted to touch God's face. Scripture tells us that they were near the tabernacle. They likely did not light their incense with the fire from heaven but were bringing strange fire. If they had used the fire from the altar, they still would not have been consecrated to approach the holy of holies. When they continued to approach the holy of holies with strange fire, they were drawn into the presence of God like the sons of Aaron, who were also in disobedience but longed to be near God. Like the sons of Aaron, I believe they received what the Talmud teaches is the divine kiss and were brought into the presence of God.

Fire has always been a symbol of the divine, passionate love of God. The fire may have consumed their bodies but they were drawn into the presence of God. Their demise was not the result of rebellion like the followers of Korach. Their demise was the divine kiss; they saw the "Face of God," and their spirits could not remain in their bodies. They had to leave their bodies to be joined with their Creator. We say they died. That word "died" is very misleading; their bodies ceased but they did not cease to exist, so they did not die.

A Christian will never die. That is, if you use the word "death" in the context of separation from God. We will never be separated from God. We will be separated from this corrupt, sinful body but that is not death. It is to the unbeliever to die, for that separates the unbeliever from the only possible link to God, and thus, they do die.

Many people may not agree with me, but I think these 250 men did not reject God; they acted in disobedience by seeking to draw near to Him in a way that was forbidden during their lifetime. As a result, they were raptured. Yes, I believe all believers are raptured. It's not quite like being taken to heaven in a physical body, but who wants to spend eternity in this broken-down shell? What a joy it would be to get raptured out of this old shell and into the presence of God.

People call the rapture "the blessed hope." Indeed, being raptured is the blessed hope, but not necessarily the end-times rapture before a seven-year tribulation. What is the difference between getting raptured in this old, corrupt body and being presented to God in a new body rather than just leaving this shell on earth and appearing before God in a new body? In my opinion, it is one and the same. Appearing before God in body or out of body? Even the apostle Paul did not know the difference, *"And I know such a man—whether in the body or out of the body I do not know, God knows"* (2 Corinthians 12:3 NKJV). Paul paid a visit to paradise, and he did not even know if he was in the body or out of the body. Can you believe that? You don't even know if you left your body or not. So, what difference does it make if you are raptured before the tribulation, or you pass from this world in a natural cause and your spirit leaves your body to be joined with a new body? Same thing, is it not? Why is the concept of the rapture such a big deal? Ultimately, we will all be raptured, and in the long run, we won't even notice any difference. I believe that despite the disobedience of these 250 men, they did not reject God; therefore, God raptured them.

The rabbinical teaching on the divine kiss is dying without any agony and fear. In fact, it is dying without even realizing you died. The presence of God becomes so real, He is so close, that your spirit just does not want to stay in your body any longer and decides to leave. You can't get much closer to a rapture than that.

23

UMBILICAL CORD

*"God is a Spirit: and they that worship him must worship
him in spirit and in truth."*
—John 4:24

In this verse, Jesus is speaking to a Samaritan woman. The
Samaritans were from the Northern District of Palestine, which
was once the Northern Kingdom of Israel. The Jews were taken
into captivity by the Assyrians. Later, the Southern Kingdom of
Judah was taken into captivity by Babylon, who had conquered
the Assyrians. The Jews were allowed to return to their homeland
during the Persian Empire. Those who were from the Northern
Kingdom returned to the Northern territory but started to assim-
ilate into the population of foreigners who had moved in when
the Jews were taken captive. Thus, while the Southern Kingdom
of Judah remained relatively pure, the Northern Jews began to
intermarry and adapt their Jewish beliefs to those of the foreign
gods. Yet, they still maintained much of their Jewish beliefs; only

it became a hodgepodge of other religions. As a result, they were barred from worshipping in the temple located in the Southern Judean area.

The Northern group had just built their place of worship. There was much debate among the Samaritans as to whether it was proper for a Jew to worship at this other site, as they did recognize that Hebrew law called explicitly for just one place of worship. The Samaritan woman asked which place of worship was acceptable to God. This question showed that she sincerely desired to connect with the God of her people.

Following Jesus's theme that the laws, temple, and worship were all matters of the heart, He said that she did not understand what worship was, for worship is not a place or a physical act; it is an act of the heart and spirit. God is a spirit, and you *worship him in spirit and in truth.*

Commentators can wax lyrical about what it means to worship in the spirit but they devote very little time to this worshipping in truth. They say that it means understanding what true worship is. Some say to worship with correct doctrine. Others say it is to worship God only and no other god alongside the true God, which would fit for the Samaritans who clung to their belief in God Jehovah but also inserted worship with other gods just to be on the safe side.

If worship is not a physical action, then much of what we call worship is not worship. Playing music, singing, dancing, and shouting is not praise and worship. These are merely manifestations of praise, but they are not praise in themselves. Genuine praise is a matter of the spirit.

In Aramaic, the word for spirit, *rauch,* refers to the Holy Spirit. There is the preposition *Beth,* which indicates in, on, or through. Jesus is saying the Holy Spirit must lead all worship. So, the pastor does not lead in worship, and the worship leader or worship team does not lead in worship; it is the Holy Spirit that leads the worship service. If the Holy Spirit leads you to sing, you sing; if He leads you to shout, you shout; if He leads you to dance, you dance. If He leads you to meditate quietly, you meditate.

What if the worship leader instructs everyone to sing, but you don't feel led to sing? Let me ask you a question. If you don't feel led to stand or sing, but you do anyway, why do you do it? Only you can answer, but many do it because they are told to, and don't want to disappoint the pastor or worship leader. Some may do it so people will not question their spirituality. Some may do it because they want to show they are genuinely loyal members of the congregation. I have heard of pastors who would call members of their church into their office and warn them that they must follow them or the worship leader in worship. If the members refused and chose a worship style that differed from the rest of the congregation, they would not be welcomed in the church. The pastor wants unity; to them, that means everyone is doing the same thing.

Do you ever wonder why, when you see Jews praying or otherwise worshipping God, they wear a prayer shawl? They do that so they are not influenced by other worshippers. They worship as a body because they can feel that unity of the body, but they realize worship is still a very personal and private matter, so they wear the prayer shawl to worship God privately, yet in a group.

When people worship according to the instruction of a worship leader or pastor, they need to ask themselves, are they doing it because they are told to and want to please their leaders? If that is the case, they are not worshipping God because they are not worshipping in *sherara'*.

In Aramaic, this word for "truth" is *sherara*, a word for an umbilical cord. The umbilical cord is what directly attaches the mother to the baby. Through that umbilical cord, the baby is nourished and even given life by the mother. When we don't follow the lead of the Holy Spirit but seek to please a pastor, worship

192 *What the Rabbis Know That I Never Learned in Church*

leader, or even fellow believers in our worship, we have detached ourselves from the umbilical cord, which connects us to the spiritual nourishment from God. Since we are trying to please a leader, we receive spiritual nourishment from that leader because we want their approval over God's approval.

I do not use a prayer shawl or a *tallit* as I am not Jewish, and many Jews would be offended if I were to use one. However, I recognize the reason for the tallit as a way of establishing a *sherara* or an umbilical cord to God. One must examine their hearts in this matter, but I often wonder how much of our worship services are truly worship to God. If we do not worship in *sherara'*, truth, our worship becomes an abomination to God.

24

VERY NEARLY

"Then Agrippa said to Paul,
'You almost persuade me to become a Christian.'"
—Acts 26:28 (NKJV)

Before I met my first rabbi or even entered a Jewish synagogue, I took an elective class in Jewish History during my first year of Bible college. I have sat through countless college classes on an undergraduate, graduate, and post-graduate level, but there was never a class that had such a profound impact on me than this class. I realized from this class that many of my questions regarding my Christian faith and my study of God's Word could be answered within the context of Judaism and its history.

I have always loved the story of King Agrippa and how Paul almost persuaded him to become a Christian. Whenever my father gave the message at the rescue mission in Chicago that he helped found, he would ask me to play an invitation hymn on the piano at the conclusion, and I would play that old hymn: "Almost Persuaded."

Then one day, I heard a sermon that blew the wind out of my sails. The preacher said that in Greek, this really meant that King Agrippa was *not* almost persuaded to become a Christian. Instead, he was telling Paul, "Do you think you could persuade me to become a Christian with such a little argument?" I was devastated and swore that one day I would study Greek and figure this out for myself.

Actually, it has yet to be figured out. You will find as many different interpretations that say King Agrippa was almost persuaded or as those that assert he was not persuaded by Paul's arguments. In Greek, *En oligo me peitheis,* which is rendered as, "With so little me do you persuade." Well, that is one way to translate it from Greek. I translate it as, "Except for a very little I am persuaded." That could be rendered in English as, "You have nearly convinced me that Christianity is true." The argument is strong from both sides. But let's check this out in Aramaic, which reads: *baqalil madam maphim,* which could read, "It is very near that you persuade me."

Ok, I am fudging on this translation; it could also read that King Agrippa is saying the opposite. So, what is it? Was he almost persuaded, or was he not moved and considered Paul's arguments very weak? There is no way to be sure from the Greek or Aramaic languages. So, let's look at the context and what little we know about King Agrippa. To do this, I must reflect on my studies in Jewish History. Could King Agrippa have had a softened heart for God? There is something very revealing in the prior verse where Paul states, *"King Agrippa, do you believe the prophets? I know that you do believe"* (Acts 26:27 NKJV). Paul would never be so bold as to tell a king what he believes or not, so King Agrippa must have made statements that indicated he believed the prophets, or maybe he was just pretending to be a believer in the prophets.

Let's go a bit into the history of the kings of Judea before and after Jesus walked the earth. Around 134–104 BCE, about a hundred years before Jesus was born, Judea conquered Edom and forced the Edomites to convert to Judaism. The Edomites were descended from Esau, Jacob's twin brother. Over the next 100 years, the Edomites gradually integrated into the Judean nation, reaching some high-ranking positions. The Edomite Antipas was appointed governor of Edom, and his son Antipater was the chief advisor to the Hasmonean dynasty, which established a co-ruling government over Judea with the Seleucidan who was established by Alexander the Great and defeated by the Maccabeans of Chanukah fame.

However, John Hyrcanus of the Hasmonean dynasty, who was an Edomite, worked his way into becoming a high priest and managed to establish a good relationship with the Roman Empire, which was extending their influence over Judea about fifty years before Jesus was born. This came after their conquest of Syria. During this time, a civil war broke out between the Jews and the Edomite Hasmonean dynasty, which Rome quelled. Julius Caesar appointed Antipas as governor and Antipater as chief advisor to John Hyrcanus II. Antipater was the father of Herod the Great, who was an Edomite and convert to Judaism. Followers of Herod were called Herodians and declared Herod the Great to be the King of the Jews. This started a conflict where the Pharisees sought to restore the kingdom to the line of David, and the Herodians wanted to keep the house of Herod ruling. After Herod was removed from office by the Roman government, there was a brief interval before the Herodians persuaded Rome to allow the grandson of Herod Agrippa I to be king, whom King Agrippa II followed. His father, Agrippa I, in order to please the Jews, had James, the son of Zebedee beheaded, and even tried to kill Peter. (See Acts 12:1–2). Tensions were rising between Rome and the Jews, and this Christian faction was not helping.

King Agrippa II was educated in Rome and was well-tutored in Jewish law and traditions. He wanted to win the favor of Jewish authorities. He was Edomite by ethnicity, and Jewish by faith. The Jews hated his grandfather, Herod the Great, because of his leanings to the Roman government. There was a great division between the Sadducees, who wanted greater influence from the Roman government, and the Pharisees, who wanted complete independence from Rome. The Pharisees were the most powerful group in Judea, but Rome was the most powerful influence.

In the seventeenth year of King Agrippa II's reign, during the reign of Nero, war was beginning to break out with Rome. Agrippa tried desperately to keep the Jews from revolting against Rome and failed. This was about the time that Paul met with King Agrippa. War broke out between Rome and the Jews, and King Agrippa sent 2,000 soldiers to aid the Roman general Vespasian, thus saving himself. He later accompanied Titus on some of his campaigns after the Jewish war of seven years between 66–73 AD, where the Jews were forced to scatter throughout the world. The temple and Jerusalem were laid in ruins by the Romans. The Romans executed the apostle Paul during the war between the Romans and the Jews. Although a Christian, he was still considered a Jew by Rome, but as a Christian, it did give Rome some pause to consider a faction of the Jews that were not nationalist. The Pharisees, of which Paul was, would make him a nationalist, which was a threat to Rome, but a Pharisee converting to this new sect might have been intriguing to Rome as a way to avert war.

Could it be that with the war pending, King Agrippa might have seen a path to a solution to the Jewish problem with Rome? Could he even consider being a Christian to influence others to follow and maybe divert a war? I guess we will never know. As far as King Agrippa's heart? Was he tender to God or just politically minded? That we will never know either in this world; one day, however, we will know.

25

THE ROLE OF WOMEN

"For God is not the author of confusion, but of peace, as in all churches of the saints. Let your women keep silence in the churches: for it is not permitted unto them to speak; but they are commanded to be under obedience, as also saith the law."
—1 Corinthians 14:33–34

"And Hannah answered and said, No, my lord, I am a woman of a sorrowful spirit: I have drunk neither wine nor strong drink, but have poured out my soul before the LORD."
—1 Samuel 1:15

The Southern Baptists take 1 Corinthians 14:33–34 literally. One argument, aside from an alleged biblical argument by Paul, is that the Orthodox Jewish synagogue excludes women from their services, and only men pray and worship in the synagogue. Such an argument shows a lack of comprehension behind the Jewish understanding of the role of women.

Did the Jews traditionally consider women inferior to men? No, far from it. Jews learned how to pray from a woman named Hannah who lived 3,000 years ago. This is found in the book of 1 Samuel, chapter 1. She wept before the Lord in the temple, pleading for a child. Along came High Priest Eli, great-grandson of Aaron, a man who was considered to be the most holy man in Israel. He was steeped in the divine mysteries of the temple. He mistook this ultimate prayer, a prayer where this woman is pouring her heart out to God in tears, and assumed she is drunk.

The whole model of prayer in Judaism is feminine; men don't like to cry. They don't like to appear helpless or express their inner selves. On top of that, men do not do it when women are around, so women were separated to allow men greater freedom to pray. In the Semitic mindset, women rule when it comes to prayer.

How about worship? Well, when the children of Israel crossed the Red Sea, the men sang, but it was the women who had a regular Pentecostal meltdown. They played cymbals and danced. Again, in worship women ruled. In the Song of Solomon, it is the woman's voice that predominates the book. The indwelling presence of God is called the *Shechinah*, which is a feminine element. God invests Himself in His creation to give it life, and He passed that honor unto women. The word for "mountain" in Hebrew is *har*. If you put it in a feminine form, it is *harah*, which means a pregnant woman. *Harah* is a play off the word *har*, not because a pregnant woman gains weight due to the pregnancy and unborn child, but because God manifested Himself on top of a mountain, Mt. Sinai. The closer someone came to the top of Mt. Sinai, the closer they came to God. A pregnant woman was considered very close to God, even having special knowledge of Him, for God was forming a life inside her. A woman was also considered to contain holiness within themselves alone, which men could only achieve in a *minyan*, a group of ten.

The Role of Women 201

Orthodox women do not sit in the main auditorium of the synagogue with the men nor do they attend the midrash with the men, because they are considered more spiritual than men. It is believed and taught in the Talmud that women are given a greater measure of spiritual insight because they must spend their time raising their children to fear God. Men must study the Torah among themselves to catch up with the women.

Women tend to let their emotions influence them. Men follow more with their mind than their emotions. This creates a balance in the physical world. Yet, there is a danger of going too far with order and too far with disorder. A man and woman are to work together for a balance. Yes, you need order in running the business of the church. Men were passing that job onto women in Paul's day and the women were at each other's throats over whether to have black olives or green olives for the fellowship dinner. (I witnessed that specific argument when I was a pastor).

It is very unlikely that Paul was addressing the worship service in 1 Corinthians. He was addressing the business aspect of the church. The churches followed the synagogue model where women were kept separate from the men because they did not require the time to study the Torah and because men needed to freely express themselves to God. As I mentioned earlier, they were not prone to express themselves when women were around. Also, as indicated, it was believed that women had a special knowledge of God. They were to spend their time raising children and could not spend the time men did in studying the Torah. Yet women were respected for their knowledge. According to an article I read by an orthodox rabbi, this is clearly played out in the story of Hannah.

When the High Priest Eli accused her of drunkenness she said, "Lo, Adonai"—No, my lord. Can you imagine saying something like that to the pope? You would have to go through a dozen diplomatic channels to correct the pope, if you even got that far. Here is a common woman declaring to the high priest of God that

202 *What the Rabbis Know That I Never Learned in Church*

he is wrong. How insolent could she get? Yet, he not only believed her, but basically admitted he was wrong by blessing her. A man would never get away with that with a high priest. This high priest respected this woman because he understood she had a relationship with God that was much different than his.

If you closely examine the culture of the first century, the culture of Semitic women, and the nature of Judaism itself, you will get a different understanding of 1 Corinthians. You will find that women are not considered inferior but would be much better at running worship and praise than organizing the Saturday potluck.

So, why would Paul tell women to keep silent in the church if women were respected and honored for their spiritual insight? The word "silent" in Aramaic is *shataq*, and this is really a word for ceasing to argue. Paul was not telling women not to preach or teach; he was instructing them to not argue.

I remember a guy telling me how he and his wife were leaving a parking space in their car and he accidentally bumped the car behind him. He got out and found there was no damage but there was a large brute of a guy glaring at him who barked, "Next time why don't you park in my front seat." The little guy immediately apologized and said how sorry he was. However, his wife had jumped out of their car and started telling her husband, "Why are you letting him get away with that? You didn't damage his car; I would not put up with that attitude. He should accept your apology." My friend turned to his wife and said, "Hush, honey, I will take care of this. Just be quiet." He was telling his wife to be *shataq*, to not argue.

I watched a fantasy movie the other night, about a family of therianthropes; that is, humans who can shapeshift into animals. The husband and father was able to turn into a dog. He was portrayed as a caring and loyal provider for the family. The two teenage children could change into predatory animals such as a wolf and coyote. We did not learn until the end of the movie what animal

The Role of Women 203

the wife and mother would change into. At the movie's conclusion, the children were being pursued by the police, and suddenly, a big angry bear appeared—that was momma. Fear did not really appear until momma bear came on the scene. Nobody wants to mess with momma bear.

Women tend to express their emotions more than men, and they can be very defensive of their families. Hannah demonstrates how a woman can be very emotional when pleading for her family. The synagogue was a place for prayer. The study of God's Word was done in a separate room after prayer called a midrash. This was usually reserved only for men, but in the early church as it was forming doctrines regarding the role of Jesus and His work of salvation, women were invited to join. Women were participating in the midrash. However, Paul discovered it was not working out too well as the midrash would often talk about personal matters, and women would get very defensive if they felt their family was being slighted. Arguments would arise. Paul was saying, "Hey, wait until you get home to discuss these personal matters and just *shataq*," that is, do not argue when discussing doctrine.

> *Let the sinners be consumed out of the earth, and let the wicked be no more. Bless thou the* Lord, *O my soul. Praise ye the* Lord.   (Psalm 104:35)

> *Let your women keep silence in the churches: for it is not permitted unto them to speak; but they are commanded to be under obedience, as also saith the law. And if they will learn any thing, let them ask their husbands at home: for it is a shame for women to speak in the church.*
>   (1 Corinthians 14:34–35)

One of the students in my Aramaic translation class shared with me a passage from the Talmud Berakoth 10a. There were once some highwaymen (thieves) who caused Rabbi Meir much

204 *What the Rabbis Know That I Never Learned in Church*

trouble. Rabbi Meir then prayed that the thieves should die. However, his wife Valeria (*Beruria* in Aramaic, meaning pureness, clearness, bright, and innocent) said to her husband, "How do you reason that God would permit such a prayer?" Rabbi Meir replied to his wife that it is written, "Let the sinners (*chatta'im*) come to an end." *Chatta'im* is an adjective rightly rendered as sinners. This is the way it is written in the Masoretic text. However, his wife responded, "In the Sefer Torah [Torah scrolls], the word is *chot'im* and is a present participle. If you look at the context you find at the end it says, 'let the wicked be no more.' Since all sin will cease, there will be no more wicked. So, you should rather pray for them that they repent."

What struck me as strange is that the husband, a rabbi, did not rebuke his wife and say, "Who are you to instruct me on the Torah? You are just a woman and not a scholar like me." Instead, he changed his prayer as she suggested. He prayed not that God would kill these men but instead that He would bring them to repentance. This woman obviously was well-versed in Hebrew grammar and studied the Torah scrolls as well as the Masoretic text, possibly more than her husband, a rabbi.

For two thousand years, the church has taught that women were to keep silent in the church and are not to teach men. This is so contradictory to the teachings of Judaism and Paul. How could Paul have said that women are not to teach men when the Talmud clearly gives us an example of a woman instructing her husband, a rabbi of all things?

For one thing, Judaism clearly teaches in the Talmud that a woman can instruct her husband in the Torah and examples are given when she does, as we find in Berakoth 10a. That would mean we either interpret Paul wrongly or there might be a little difference in nuance in the translations.

The purpose of this chapter is to examine Valeria's rendering of Psalm 104:35. She is right, of course. In the Christian world, the Masoretic text is almost consider inspired. The Masoretic text was not developed until 700 years after the birth of Christ. Before that time, the *niqqud*—which means dotting or pointings indicating vowels and dageshes—were not found in the Sefer Torah. This was introduced by a Jewish sect known as the Masorites, who developed it to preserve the biblical Hebrew. The Masoretic text, as it has become known, turn the Torah into a more precise document. In their aim for precision, they took the ambiguity right out of the text. We in the Western world demand that two plus two equals four and the Masoretic text gives us that. However, that does not mean the Masorites were always correct in their conclusion. Many rabbis do not trust or revere the Masoretic text like we Christians do. The Masoretic text is even considered by some to be just a paraphrase of the Holy Scriptures. The Sefer Torah is considered the true inspired text.

When I was in Bible college and seminary, the Masoretic Text always won out over the Septuagint in any dispute. The Septuagint is a Greek translation of the Old Testament. Forget the fact that it is almost a thousand years older than the Masoretic text and thus should be more accurate. We Western Christians just love our languages to be precise. It was discovered from the Dead Sea Scrolls that the Septuagint is more accurate than the Masoretic text.

We should look at Psalms 104:35 not as instruction to pray that our enemies be consumed, killed, or in Hebrew *tammu*, which means to come to an end or vanish. Instead like Valeria said, we should pray for our enemies that they repent. Jesus teaches the same thing, *"Bless them that curse you, and pray for them which despitefully use you"* (Luke 6:28).

So what about this business of women keeping silent in the church and only learning from their husbands? According to this verse in 1 Corinthians, women should not even attend church as they are to learn only from their husbands, which means to me no learning from a pastor. Of course, no pastor is

206 *What the Rabbis Know That I Never Learned in Church*

going to tell a woman to stay home from church and let their husbands teach them. They are the pastor, after all, and they do all the teaching.

We need to understand that when this was written the church was modeled after the synagogue of the first century. In Hebrew, the synagogue is the *bet knesset*, house of assembly, or *bet tefilla*, house of prayer. It is a place for prayer and reading of the Torah. It is not necessarily a place of worship. The Halakha teaches that worship can be carried out anywhere and anytime where there is a *minya*, an assembly of ten Jews. Some synagogues have separate rooms called the *beth midrash*, or house of study.

When trying to understand 1 Corinthians 14, we make the mistake of picturing our modern twenty-first century church instead of a first-century synagogue. We call our church services worship services. The synagogue is a house of prayer. The primary purpose of the synagogue is a consecrated place to pray to God. A typical service in the synagogue will consist of prayers and reading from the Torah, following a weekly Torah selection called a *parshah*, which is Hebrew for portion. Then the rabbi will give a brief commentary on that Torah portion. There is also a reading from the Haftorah, which comes from one of the other books of the Old Testament. There is a lot of standing and bowing, showing respect for the Word of God and honoring the Word of God.

The rabbi is not a preacher or even a teacher as we consider a teacher in the Western world. He is the leader of his congregation who facilitates rather than teaches. He is a counselor in the Torah and a resource person for Torah knowledge and understanding.

Let's examine this passage in 1 Corinthians in light of this structure of the synagogue. Paul is most likely referencing the *beth midrash*, where members of the congregation assemble after a time of prayer. It is a far less formal open forum where members discuss

The Role of Women 207

the Torah and Talmud. Women were allowed into this room in the first century Christian synagogue/church.

The problem arises because first century marriages suffered from much of the afflictions witnessed in marriages today. Conflicts will naturally arise when two people live together and share a life together, including finances, plans, children, and so forth. Disagreements happen in all marriages. Some are mild and some can get extremely violent. Grudges develop, and when the opportunity to publicly air the frustrations over a mate arise, some will do it. So here you have a midrash or Bible study where a husband and wife are attending and the topic goes to finances. Suddenly a wife might say, "You know what my dimwit of a husband spent our last shekels on?" Then the mud hits the fan, and the husband says, "You know what my foolish wife did last week?" Soon, there is no Bible study but an airing of everyone's grievances over their mates.

Paul is not saying that *women* should keep silent, but the word in Aramaic, *anatta*, indicates *wives* should keep silent. Big difference. They are to keep silent in the *edita* or *'adah* in its Semitic root. An *'adah* is loosely rendered as church, but it is not a church in today's terminology. If Paul meant a church, he would have used the word *qahal*, which means an assembly or congregation of people. *'Adah*, however, is a legal term for a place where witnesses testify. This is a place where everyone is free to express what they have experienced and seen. It would be a specific place and time. Hence, this is likely the first-century form of the *beth midrash* where everyone can share their opinions and ideas as to the meaning behind a passage of Scripture. Women are to keep *shetheq* during this time. Yes, it can mean silent, but silent in the sense of not arguing a point, not rebuking, not calling someone a toad and blasting them out of the water.

This does not mean that women were not allowed to speak or teach others. They were not allowed to rebuke their husbands in a public forum when discussing the Holy Scriptures. So, what does it mean when it says if they want to learn anything, let them ask their husband? I'm glad you asked that question. The word "learn" is *yileph* in Aramaic, which can be used for learning but it is more of an apprenticeship in the sense of getting accustomed to procedures and protocol. In other words, women being allowed to attend a midrash with men was something new and they were not familiar with the way of things, the unspoken codes.

It would be similar to a freshman congressperson. The first few months in office they are not familiar with how things are run and often unintentionally break protocols and procedures. Usually, a senior congressional person will take that freshman under their wing and teach them the proper way of things. This is likely what Paul meant about a woman learning from her husband. The husband was to teach her how to conduct herself in a midrash. The husband was to mentor her, so to speak, in the ways of *namusa*. *Namusa* loosely means laws but really means procedures or customs.

In other words, the wives are not allowed to speak but rather (*ela* in Aramaic) they are to be subject to the customs of the congregation. If anything, their husbands should mentor them (in the customs of the congregation) "for it is a shame." That word "shame" in Aramaic is *behatta*, which comes from a Semitic root for the bending of a tree from the pressure of the wind. It has the idea of being so pressured that you end up creating confusion. In other words, there may be some deep discussion on a passage of Scripture, and the woman, because of her lack of experience, may speak out about something totally unrelated and cause the whole point of the discussion to become confusing.

The context also seems to suggest a reference to prophesying. There is a time and place to prophecy. The women were choosing the wrong time to prophecy during a midrash, causing confusion.

To interpret these verses as a call for women to keep silent in the church, not teach men, humbly shut up, and meekly sit in church while the men run everything may not be what Paul is referencing at all.

26

CAPITAL PUNISHMENT

"They say unto him, Master, this woman was taken in adultery, in the very act. Now Moses in the law commanded us, that such should be stoned: but what sayest thou? This they said, tempting him, that they might have to accuse him. But Jesus stooped down, and with his finger wrote on the ground, [as though he heard them not]."
—John 8:4–6
That last part in brackets, "He heard them not," is not in the original inspired text. However, it is included in the King James Version.

How was it that the Pharisees were tempting Jesus with the woman taken in adultery and that His response would give them grounds to accuse him? The word "tempt" in Aramaic is *nasi*, which has the idea of trying something out, or taking it for a test drive. The Pharisees wanted Jesus to take the Mosaic law out for a test drive so to speak. Adultery was one of the Mosaic laws that carried a capital punishment. Yet, after years of suffering in captivity and experiencing so much death from executions, the Jews could not stomach the idea of putting a human to death. They created many checks and balances that required a lengthy due process before anyone could get executed, to the point where a capital crime rarely ended in death. The Pharisees were literally telling Jesus, who was continually condemning oral laws and tradition by man, that if He followed the strict letter of the law they should immediately stone this woman. If Jesus said to stone her according to the Jewish law, then they could tell Jesus that their traditions were more humane than the strict letter of the law and bring Jesus before the Sanhedrin on charges of breaking religious law. Instead, Jesus caught them off guard by appealing to the mercy of God.

I was reading in the Talmud in Sanhedrin 2a-b. As I read this, I once again wondered how Christians remain so aloof to the teachings of the ancient rabbis and sages. They instead formulate their own opinions on difficult passages when it is not difficult if you give some attention to the ancient Jewish culture. This is one of many examples of Christians who seem to just teach what some other teacher taught, who learned it from another teacher. Few ever really step out of their box and go to a Jewish source for answers. After 2,000 years, we Christians still ponder over passages that were easily understood by the Jewish people in the first century.

I have heard many Christians try to explain this passage in John 8:1–11 in ways that just leave me with more questions. What did Jesus write in the ground? How were they testing Jesus by quoting the Torah and saying the woman should be stoned? Why did these so-called blood-thirsty Pharisees who were apparently very anxious to put this woman to death suddenly find that they had to walk away when Jesus said, *"He that is without sin among you, let him first cast a stone at her"* (John 8:7)? Finally, what did the woman mean no one was accusing her? She was caught red-handed. Why would someone not accuse her and stone her according to the law?

I have heard dozens of explanations. Take for example the fact that Jesus wrote in the ground. The Bible does not tell us what He wrote. Maybe because it was obvious to any Jew. I have heard explanations that Jesus wrote the names of the men who committed adultery with this woman. That seems to be very popular because, "Ha, ha, Jesus really caught them red-handed." It took a rabbi to explain to me what Jesus wrote, and it was much more clever and more profound than catching them red-handed.

Around 300 AD Constantine conquered all of Europe and wanted to consolidate his kingdom. To do this, he needed to have a unified religion. Thus, he began to universalize Christianity with other pagan religions, bringing in pagan worship practices. The Jewish Christians rebelled. Well, rebellion was one thing Constantine would not tolerate so he threw all the Jews out of the church, including two thousand years of Jewish culture, traditions, and books like the Talmud. The church then declared the Jews were Christ killers and that became the Orthodox teaching passing into Protestantism with the likes of Martin Luther, who took a dim view of the Jews. It was not until 1962 when Pope John attended a mass where the priest was performing his obligatory Good Friday sermon condemning the Jews as Christ killers. The pope was aghast that the church still clung to this dogma. He declared the Jews were not Christ killers and the priests were never again to preach a sermon against the Jews.

You see, Pope John was a scholar who studied the Talmud. I believe he read what I read in Sanhedrin 2a-b and realized that the Jews as a whole in the first century were anything but Christ killers. Oh, to be sure, there was a small segment of Jews who wanted to put Jesus to death—and later to put Christians to death, like Saul who soon became the apostle Paul—but it was a very small segment.

214 *What the Rabbis Know That I Never Learned in Church*

Let me quote to you from the Talmud something that was in practice during the day of Jesus:

> Monetary matters are decided by a court of three judges … capital crimes {like adultery} by a tribunal of twenty-three judges. … From where is this derived? For it is written Numbers 35:24–25: "The community shall judge … and the community shall save"—we need a community of judges arguing to convict the accused, and a community of judges arguing to exonerate him. Thus, we have twenty (a "community" indicating a minimum of ten, as per Numbers 14:27. A conviction requires a majority of two (as per Exodus 23:2), and a court of law cannot have an even number of judges; thus we need twenty-three judges so that there should be a majority of two over the ten "saving" judges, and another judge so that the court should not be even-numbered)." (Sanhedrin 2 a-b)

Twenty-three judges were necessary for a conviction of a capital crime like adultery. The Pharisees who took this woman to Jesus knew the law very well and knew Jesus could not condemn this woman under present Jewish law, for you needed a court of twenty-three judges. Aside from this were many other hoops to jump through, such as the nature of witnesses and their testimonies, so that by the first century the Jews made it virtually impossible to execute anyone. That is why Jesus had to be tried before Pilate. By the time the Jews returned from their captivity, they could no longer stomach the idea of killing someone even if he was a criminal. They did like we have done in our country—create so many checks and balances, appeals, and rules of law that it would take years for a person to be executed if they are executed at all.

These Pharisees were not trying to kill this woman; they were trying to put Jesus in a tight situation where He had to admit that the oral law, the traditions of the fathers, carried as much weight as the Torah. You see, they believed that whatever was bound on earth by two or three in agreement would be bound in heaven. The Talmud teaches that where two or three are gathered together in agreement, the divine presence is in their midst. In other words, where two or three agree that watching a football game on Saturday is in violation of the Sabbath law of keeping the day holy, then they would bind this on earth and it would therefore be bound in heaven. If they decided to make the Super Bowl an exception and if two or three were in agreement, the ban on watching football on the Sabbath would be released on earth and in heaven. Hence, the authority of the tradition of the fathers or the Talmud.

But Jesus was teaching against the authority of the Tradition of the Fathers and many of the laws of the Tradition of the Fathers or the Talmud, so these Pharisees were testing Jesus, trying to back Him in a corner where He had to admit to the authority of the Tradition of the Fathers or appear like some heartless, vindictive teacher totally out of character with the true nature of a loving God, not to mention a conviction from the Sanhedrin resulting in excommunication.

However, Jesus did them one better. I asked a rabbi what he thought Jesus wrote in the ground and he laughed. "Must I, a Jew, explain your own New Testament to you? Jesus most likely wrote a *Yod* and *Hei* to represent the feminine aspect of God. That is the loving, benevolent, caring nature of God. He could not speak that name nor write it, but he could write the *Yod Hei* and the Pharisees knew what He meant. Jesus appealed to the merciful side of God, the side that forgives. Had he written an *Aleph Mem* for Elohim it would show the masculine side, the disciplinary side that would condemn the woman. Instead, Jesus appealed to the mercy of God." He may have continued to write out a Scripture passage, "*Come now, and let us reason together,…though your sins be as scarlet, they shall be as white as snow*" (Isaiah 1:18). Simply put, Jesus told the Pharisees, "We all deserve to die for our sins. If there is anyone of you who is sinless and does not need the mercy of God, let him cast the first stone." Of course, they all had to leave, for they knew they needed God's mercy as much as this poor woman.

27

GATES OF HELL

"And I say also unto thee, That thou art Peter,
and upon this rock I will build my church; and the gates of
hell shall not prevail against it."
—Matthew 16:18

I've listened to many arguments over whether the rock upon which the church is built is Peter, Jesus, or Peter's confession of faith. Yet, no one seems to argue or show any concern as to what the gates of hell that will not prevail against the church really are.

Our first assumption is that it is the hell of fire and brimstone, meaning the forces of hell itself and the demonic beings cannot prevail against the church. What bothers me about this is why call it the *gates* of hell and not the *forces* of hell? How can a gate prevail against anything except someone trying to get in or out. Why would the church try to get into hell and why would the church try to get out of hell if not in it in the first place?

218 *What the Rabbis Know That I Never Learned in Church*

I don't think "hell" is the best rendering here. In Greek it is the word *hadou* or *hades*, which is a place where the departed spirits go until the day of resurrection. In Aramaic, it is the word *sheol*, which is the grave; again, a place where the dead go. The word "gates" is what creates a problem. The word in Greek is *pylai*, which is a door or entrance from which you enter or exit. The word for "prevail" is *katischuo*, which is a word for overpowering someone, getting the upper hand. The door of the grave or the place of the dead spirits will not overpower the church?

The word in Aramaic for "gate" is *tara'a*, which is an opening or a portal, a passageway. The word for "prevail" is *chasan*, which means to subdue or overpower just like in the Greek. Still even in the Aramaic, it does not make sense. How can a portal to the grave or place of the dead overcome the church? They seem to be unrelated, unless we go with the traditional explanation that Jesus is referring to the powers of hell, but I am troubled over why He just does not say the powers of hell. Why speak in cryptic terms like the gates of hell?

The term "gates of hell" had to be very familiar to the Jews of the first century. Indeed it was. I found numerous references to this in the Jewish Talmud. But the one I think is appropriate for this Scripture passage is found in Baba Bathra 84a: "Is not the sun red at sunrise and at sunset? It is red at sunrise, because it passes by the roses of the garden of Eden, at sunset, because it passes the gate of *sheol*." In other words, the sun is red as it sets in the West because it reflects the fires of *sheol*, but is red as it rises due to the reflection the roses of the garden of Eden. The garden of Eden is said to be the resting place of the souls of the righteous and *sheol* is the resting place of the souls of the unrighteous.

To the first-century Jew, the gates of hell were a symbol of the resting place of the unrighteous and death. Jesus may very well have been saying that not even death or the attacks of the unrighteous will stop the church. Or He might even be making a reference to

His death and possibly those of all the martyrs to come would not stop the church from moving forward.

Indeed, history has shown, even today, that when the church is persecuted, it only grows stronger. The church in China is the best example. Under persecution the church is united, no phonies in the church during persecution. No one plays the game when belonging to Jesus could mean prison, torture, or death. Not even the threat of death can stop the church. Any way you look at it, neither death, the attacks of the demonic, the unrighteous, or even the death of the founder of the church, Jesus Himself, cannot stop the church because Jesus conquered death.

28

FORTY DAYS FORTY YEARS

*"And they brought up an evil report of the land which they
had searched unto the children of Israel, saying,
The land, through which we have gone to search it, is a land
that eateth up the inhabitants thereof; and all the people that
we saw in it are men of a great stature."*
—Numbers 13:32

We all remember this story from Sunday school. Twelves spies went into the promised land and only two returned with a good report. Actually, all agreed that it was indeed a land flowing with milk and honey, but there were giants in the land and they felt they could not conquer that land. However, the giants were not the only thing that scared them. Before they even mentioned the giants, they mentioned something else: "a land that eats up its inhabitants."

Now let's go back to these spies. Who were they? Were they really spineless and gutless? Why would they be fearful of giants after seeing God move the waters of the Red Sea, provide manna every day, supply water from a rock, and give them victory over the Amalekites, who were far more skilled and powerful in warfare? After God's miraculous wonders, why would they still fear?

The names of these spies were listed in Numbers. I learned from rabbis not to ignore names in the Bible because they often hold secret clues to hidden messages in the Holy Scriptures. When God uses a name, He does it for a reason.

The names of these ten negative spies represent their reputations:

Shammua: One who is renowned, celebrated, famous. Today, we would say a rock star.

Shaphat: A judge, one who is wise with deep insight.

Igal: One who redeems, pays a debt for someone else

Palti: One who rescues another; a deliverer. The guy you want around if you are bullied.

Gaddiel: My fortune is in God.

Gaddi: One who cuts oneself off from something. As one who choses God over fortune.

Ammiel: I am part of God's family.

Sethur: A hiding place, one who provides shelter.

Nahbi: One who enters into the secrets of God.

Geuel: One who shows the majesty of God.

These are all superheroes, beloved, and honored. They were leaders of each of the twelve tribes who were sworn to uphold the laws of God. To do as God commanded them to do.

CALEB

The word "Caleb" could be read as two different understandings. One is that it is the word for a dog. However, you could read that first letter which is a *Kap* as the preposition like or as. Then it would read like or as your heart. Caleb was a spy with a soft, tender heart like a domesticated dog, loving, and loyal. Caleb was loyal to his people. He showed heart, and a desire to honor his deceased ancestors by crossing into the land of Hebron, the land of the giants, to inspect the graves or tombs of his ancestors to make sure they were not desecrated. None of the other spies were willing to run the risk of tending to the graves of their ancestors that they never knew. Why bother? Their ancestors were dead and gone for over a couple hundred years. However, to Caleb, those graves were his legacy; his people once dwelled in that land. I am sure Caleb tried to get others to go with him, but no one would risk it. There were, after all, giants in that land.

So, Caleb went alone. Caleb was just one of two spies who gave a good report upon their return. Caleb's tenderheartedness could not go against God's command to conquer the land, even if it looked like they were outnumbered. This was the land of his people, who were buried there. That land belonged to Caleb and his future generation. The other spies only saw the land as a place where they could live in freedom from slavery. They did not realize the promise that was given to their ancestors about that land. Otherwise, like Caleb, they too would have wanted to visited the graves of their ancestors, honor them, and renew their vows before God who had given them this land.

The tombs or graves of Caleb's ancestors were left untouched for 200 years. This must have been an incredibly emotional experience for a man with such a tender heart and love for God. No doubt God spoke to Caleb as he stood before those graves and reminded him of all the stories his mother used to tell him about his ancestors. How God prospered and protected Abraham and

His deliverance of Lot, a distant uncle, from the cities of Sodom and Gomorrah. God assured Caleb that He would be with him and his people as they entered the promised land.

Many times, when I am doubting God, when I am fearful and wondering if God would be there to protect me, I would reflect on stories of my ancestors, perhaps as Caleb did. I recall stories of my grandfather in World War I, who was in a foxhole with one of his buddies when a shell exploded. His buddy's body was torn to pieces just inches from him by that shell, but my grandfather only suffered a piece of shrapnel in one ear. The war wound lead to deafness in that ear, reminding him of God's providence. God brought him through those times.

I think of my grandmother during the depression, who went door-to-door selling home baked bread so she could make some money to feed her family. I recall how my father sold newspapers as a young boy and gave all his earnings to the family so they could eat. He kept back only enough to save for a bicycle, which he would ride to the lake. His pastor, who led him to the Lord, purchased some fishing line for him so he could catch some perch to feed his family during the depression. I recall when I was a child how my father worked as a milkman and when he was sure his family had enough to live on he would use any excess money to help establish a rescue mission in the inner city of Chicago to help feed and care for the homeless. God always provided for us; we never went without the necessities of life.

Perhaps as Caleb pondered all these family stories, his faith was strengthened and he became emboldened to return to the land of his people regardless of giants or a land that would consume the people. I can picture Caleb praying to God over the graves of his ancestors, a prayer I often raise up to God. "If You did it for that generation, You will do it for mine, I am ready to fight whatever battle You lead me into, even if it is against giants." The others spies who did not want to chance running into giants and were too

Forty Days Forty Years 225

fearful to visit the graves of their ancestors did not have the benefit of this inspiriting moment before the graves of their ancestors.

JOSHUA

Then there was another man who was also determined to fight the fight. This man was Joshua. His name was really Hosea, but just before he went out on his spying mission, God through Moses changed his name from *Hosea*—one who saves—to *Yashua*—one who will save. Funny, how God only changed the name of one spy, who also happened to give a good report. Joshua was Moses's righthand man; he climbed the mountain with Moses. When Moses was in the prayer tent, Joshua was with him, and he stayed in the tent to continue praying even after Moses left. God changed Hosea's name to *Yashua* as a sign to all the people that despite the negative report about powerful armies, God would deliver them. I think it was also a sign of the coming of another Yashua or Joshua, one who would lead all His people to another promised land. The kingdom of God by which no man can enter but through Yeshua Hamashiach—Jesus Christ—Jesus the Messiah.

All these men who were sent out to spy the land were great men. They were morally good men, righteous men, holy men, men like our television evangelists and preachers. They were the bishops, denominational superintendents, YouTube sensations, Internet wonders, writers of great Christian books, and theologians. These were men of reputation, trusted men. Men whose political counsel you would follow come election time, and who held fast on their views of eschatological doctrines.

If they said there were giants who could lop off your head, well, by golly there were giants who would lop off your head. Surely, they knew better than you what God was saying. If a majority of highly respected, credentialed men like the other ten spies said it was too dangerous to enter the promised land, then it was too dangerous. Forget the fact that God changed the name of one of the spies to "God saves" to "God will save" just before they left to spy out the land. He obviously let the name change go to his head! Forget that one of the spies, Caleb, entered the land of the giants to pay homage to their ancestors and listened to his soul-stirring testimony of what it was like to stand before the graves of their distant relatives and reflect on how God saved them in the past. No, the majority of these respected righteous men said it was too dangerous and life-threatening.

The people did not listen to that minority report from Joshua and Caleb. No more manna from heaven, and no more protection from the scorching heat of the desert from a cloud. They would work in the hot sun, plow fields, plant seeds, and harvest their own food. Their lives would no longer be sitting around studying the Torah, singing "I Like God" songs, and basking in the air conditioned cloud of glory. No, they were going to deal with armies, and with giants. They chose to listen to the mainstream lies of the ten spies: a majority report of the experts. They not only refused to enter the land, but began to whine and weep. *"It would have been better for us to serve the Egyptians than that we should die in the wilderness"* (Exodus 14:12 NKJV). They would rather be enslaved in Egypt than face the possibilities that were reported by the news of the ten spies.

God could save them from the spies, but there was something God could and would not save them from—their wills. What so frightened these spies, these men of God, these heroes? Two things: labor and insignificance. Note the words, *"a land that eateth up the inhabitants."* What does that mean? I read in Jewish literature that the people grew accustomed to miracles. They watched God usher them through the Red Sea, bring forth water from a rock, give them victory over the Amalekites, deliver them from poisonous snakes, and many other wonders. The elderly did not grow tired staying in step with the younger. Their shoes did not wear out, and they did not have to labor under the sweat of their

Forty Days Forty Years 227

brows for food. Of course, there arose leadership, heroes, celebrities, and reputations built on holiness. These were celebrated while in the wilderness and their fame and usefulness would disappear once they were in the promised land. Once there, they would have to work for their food. Their communities would be scattered and their fame forgotten. The land would eat them up. The word "eat" is 'achol in Hebrew, which means to completely consume or absorb. In other words, when people had to work for their daily bread, they would not have time to honor their rock stars. These spies would not only have to work, but their prior occupation would become insignificant. They would be the pastors clinging to their old methods, watching their congregation disappear to the new styles of worship. They would be the television preachers watching their numbers decline in favor of the cheaper podcast and YouTube personalities. They would be the Christian writers watching their book sales decline as Christian bookstores close and self-publishing floods the market with books written by anyone with a laptop.

Christians today watch in fear and horror of modern giants: ongoing political division, inflation, socialism, religious persecution, and so on. They whine and moan, "Oh, that we could go back to the way it was."

After a day's reflection, some of the people decided they were wrong and should enter the promised land and got an army together to do that very thing. But it was too little, too late. God was not with them, and they were driven back. There are many Christians today seeking to overturn the new government, but they are being driven back. Perhaps God is saying like He did four thousand years ago, "You are not ready yet. You need to return to the wilderness to learn true faith, experience revival, and reformation."

These spies spent forty days scouting out the land. They had forty days to consider how big that land was compared to their little crowded community in the wilderness where they were the rock stars. They knew they could stand out in a pond of their enclosed community, but put the people in the oceans of the promised land, and they would disappear into insignificance.

Caleb and Joshua reported that it was a good land, but it would take a lot of work to cultivate it, clear it out, build permanent homes, and then try to get rid of those giants. Perhaps the Jewish commentators are wrong, perhaps I am wrong, but I don't think these spies were afraid of the giants. Their great sin was not fear to go to battle. Their fear was being labeled "Mr. Irrelevant," the last pick of the annual NFL draft. They had one last chance to use their influence, and they did. They created a climate of fear among the people. Maybe things were not so bad in the wilderness;. Let God provide food, health care, education, money, clouds and fire to protect you night and day.

So what happened to these spies? Well, they met a very undesirable fate. The people got their wish: they got to spend the rest of their lives in the wilderness living off manna and water from the rock. There were a few who said, "Moses, we blew it. We listened to these men and now they are but ashes. We are ready. Let's go get the land." But God told Moses, "It is too late; the people are not 100% behind this, and without unity, you will have no victory. Tell them not to go. I will not, I cannot, protect them when the entire camp is in rebellion." But they were *ma'apilim*, defiant. They were like the pastors who tell their congregants, "If you don't like my sermons and style, then leave. I will build this church with people who stand behind me." That type of mindset produces cults.

No, God wanted all the people to be unified under Him. When Joshua was given leadership, God instructed everyone to submit to Joshua. If they did not, they would be put to death. As it was, there were those who stood behind Moses, those with *ma'apilim*—defiance to Moses, those who listened to their heroes, and those who followed their own path.

Those who thought they could take the land amid disunity and rebel against God Himself suffered a great defeat entering the land. God is looking for unity, but only the unity that is centered around Him and not some superstar.

Something that really stands out for me when I observe Judaism is that they are as diverse in their doctrines, theologies, and views on God as we Christians are. However, they are still Jews; they are still a family. When the chips are down, they unite. Neither orthodox, conservative, or reformed, they are first a family.

Again, the Jewish people are a role model for us Christians. We may be very diverse in our beliefs and doctrines, but we need to remember we are still all brothers and sisters in the family of God. Our survival will depend upon that unity as it does with the Jewish people.

29

JEWISH BELIEF ABOUT HEAVEN

"And Enoch walked with God: and he was not;
for God took him."
—Genesis 5:24

I remember back when I was a student at Moody Bible Institute. It was the only accredited undergraduate evangelical Christian college that had a major in Jewish Studies (formerly called Jewish Evangelism). A few years after I graduated, it was officially changed to Jewish Studies, so I feel I can honestly say I was a Jewish Studies major. It was designed for those who were called to be Jewish missionaries. However, it was the only way I could take an undergraduate class in Hebrew in a Christian environment. I could have taken Hebrew as an elective—we had a few students in my Hebrew classes do that—but you still did not get the benefit of classes about Judaism. So, I actually had a double major, Christian Education and Jewish Studies. I knew I wasn't going anywhere with a major in Jewish Evangelism.

Well, there were all of five students who were in this major, and we all had assignments to work with Jewish missions and local messianic churches, allowing us to get immersed into the Jewish faith and culture. There was one guy in our group who was a senior and was about to get his accredited degree in Jewish Evangelism. He was a dedicated student and became like a mentor to the rest of us. He would often take us the local synagogue, where we met the rabbis and learned many things about Judaism firsthand. I remember sitting in a service in the synagogue, and our mentor leaned over to me during a recitation of the Mourner's Kaddish, where they read the names of all the members who had passed on. He whispered, "This is the saddest part of the service." I asked him about it later, and he said it was so sad because they had no hope; they did not believe in heaven. I was surprised about this, and as the years passed I often wondered about this. I would ask rabbis if they believed in heaven and the usual answer would be, "Not like you believe," and then I would let the subject drop. I remember others, like a Catholic priest, telling me that Jews did not believe in heaven. In fact, this seemed to be the general belief among Christians.

Finally, I decided to really research this and find out what Jews really believed about heaven, and if they really did believe in heaven in the first place. I found it difficult to find definitive material on this subject as there is a wide variety of beliefs about life after death among Jews. It is true some Jews do not believe in an afterlife; some Jews don't even believe in God for that matter. Just like in Christianity we have a wide range of doctrine and beliefs, Jews also have a wide range of beliefs.

In Christianity, we have basically three branches: fundamentalism, evangelicalism, and liberalism.

Fundamentalists are those who take a very strict view on Scripture and hold tightly to the fundamentals of the faith like the virgin birth, water baptism by immersion, the deity of Jesus, and the Bible as the inspired and infallible Word of God. They also have strict views on things like dancing, smoking, drinking, and attending theaters, which they consider sinful. They tend to be very exclusive and will not accept anyone who is charismatic, speaking in tongues, or believes in faith healing and prophecy. They are the ones that Hollywood likes to mock as dressed in black suits, white shirts, and ties, carrying a big Scofield Bible.

Evangelicals are pretty much the same but not as strict about sins that are not mentioned in the Bible, like smoking and movies. They are not that exclusive and accept the charismatics, Pentecostals who speak in tongues and move in the gifts of spirit as fellow believers. They do hold strongly to the basic tenets of our faith such as the inspiration of Scripture, the deity of Christ, and His virgin birth. Both groups do have the common belief that salvation and the way to heaven is a choice to be made in accepting Jesus Christ as your personal Savior and surrendering your life to Him. Fundamentalists feel that you need to point to a particular time and place when you made this decision and prayed a specific prayer to receive Jesus as your Savior. Evangelicals believe that you can either point to a specific time and place where you made this decision but that this decision could have been one that you gradually came into. In other words, there may have been a specific time and place that you received Jesus as your Savior but you cannot really point to it; all you know at the present is that you are trusting in Jesus for your salvation and believing that God has covered all your sins by His blood.

Liberals will question whether the Bible is truly the inspired Word of God, whether Jesus is really God incarnate, and if He was truly virgin born. Some even question whether God exists at all. They will also question the existence of a heaven, and most do not believe in a hell. You will find these people mostly on the East and West Coasts, teaching in the religious departments of secular universities and colleges.

I mention all this to put into context the range of Jewish belief. You have Jews who don't believe in God, heaven, or hell, and those on the other end of the spectrum who do believe in God, heaven, and hell. So just as we have a wide range of beliefs in Christianity about heaven and hell—the Catholics even have a third place called purgatory—the Jews also have a wide range of beliefs in the afterlife.

Jews can be divided into three groups, like Christianity. There is Reformed Judaism, which is much like our liberals in Christianity. They will question the existence of a heaven and hell, the inspiration of Scripture, and some even question the existence of God. Then you have Conservative Jews who believe in the inspiration of Scripture or the Torah. Some consider the Holy Books like the Talmud and Midrash to be authoritative but not inspired and they believe in an afterlife. Orthodox Jews are the third group, and like Christianity, there are many divisions here as well. They are similar to the fundamentalists, and take a very strict view and understanding of the Torah and hold the Talmud and Midrash to be authoritative.

The reason so many Christians think the Jews do not believe in an afterlife is most of the Jews that Christians know are reformed, and they likely do not believe in an afterlife. So, what I will share on their view of heaven is a general understanding. But first let me share one cardinal rule about the afterlife held by all Jews.

Jews don't talk about an afterlife. This reason is very important for Christians to understand, and to seriously consider in relation to their faith. One rabbi explained to me that to talk about it, dream about, and look forward to it might cause you to serve God for selfish reasons. You will serve God not out of love but because you are trying to earn a place in the afterlife.

There is the story of a rabbi who was asked by a man if he would pray for him for a specific request. The man felt that a rabbi would likely be heard by God better than an average person. The rabbi agreed to present the man's request to God. God told the rabbi He would grant the man's request only if the rabbi would agree to forfeit his place in the afterlife. The rabbi agreed and reported to the man that God would grant his request. The rabbi then told the man the price he had to pay for the request being granted, which was to forfeit his place in the afterlife. The man objected and said, "No, rabbi, I never would have asked you to do such a thing." The rabbi responded, "You don't understand, I wanted to do it. For all my life I wondered if I was serving God just to secure a place in the afterlife. Now that I know I have no inheritance in the afterlife, I can know for certain that I serve God out of love for Him."

That is something for every Christian to ponder. Are you serving God out of love or is there something in the back of your mind that makes you think that you better be sure to attend church every Sunday, tithe, study the Bible, and even give a witness now and then, just to safeguard your home in heaven? You see, there are two reasons why salvation is a free gift, not of works. (See Ephesians 2:8–9.) One is, as Paul says, so you will not boast about your piousness. The second is that you will learn to serve God like the Jews, out of love, and not to bribe your way into heaven with good works.

To the average Jew, belief in an afterlife is fundamental to Judaism. It is a foundation stone without which the entire structure of our faith would collapse. Like Christianity, it begins with what is known in Hebrew as the *Neshamah*. This is what God breathed into man—the immortal soul that God gave to us and to no other creature in His creation. The Jews call it a spark of the divine. Everything in the natural world will decay and decompose, including our bodies in the grave. However, the soul of man, the *Neshamah*, is that eternal spark that God placed within us that makes us immortal and causes us to live forever.

Now, there is sect of the Jews, including mainly Orthodox Jewish groups like the Chabad, who believe that the creation of souls has ceased and that all souls come back to another body after it dies. That is called reincarnation. This is an old belief in Judaism that Jesus debunked in John 9 when the disciples asked who sinned that this man be born blind, he or his parents. How could the man have sinned before he was born and why would that sin cause him to be blind? This is believed to be a reference to the Jewish teaching of reincarnation during the day of Jesus, one that was questionable among many Jewish scholars and not widely believed.

As I said, Judaism is not about, "Do this and you get a ticket to heaven." The Mishnah teaches that one should not be like "servants who serve their master for a reward" (Avot 1:4). One is to follow the truth for the truth's sake. Doing God's will is not like a punch card, where the more punches you get, the better your chance of winning a ticket to heaven.

As far as the nature of heaven and what it is like, to get a biblical view of heaven is difficult in the Bible. Particularly in the Old Testament, you will not find much about heaven. But you do get a sense that there is something beyond death. Genesis 5:24 tells us that Enoch walked with God and then he was gone; God took him. Took him where? The Bible doesn't say. Abraham is told that he will go to his fathers in peace. (See Genesis 15:15.) That sounds like a specific place, but where? The Bible is silent, only that he will be with his fathers. Were his fathers not idolaters? They would surely not be in heaven. Perhaps that is just a reference to the grave. That is one reason Jews will not practice cremation and securing the right burial plot takes high priority.

I know a man who rides my disability bus. When his mother died, he went through a lot of trouble and expense to obtain a loan to have his mother's remains taken to New York to be buried in the proper place. The Bible specifically talks about Jacob's bones being brought back to be buried with his family when the Jews returned from Egypt. (See Joshua 24:32.) Perhaps that is what God meant when He said Abraham would go to his fathers. But there are other passages clearer than this that talk of an afterlife. Elijah was taken to heaven in a fiery chariot (see 2 Kings 2:11–12) and Malachi predicted that he will return in the future as the harbinger of the messianic era (Malachi 4:5–6). This indicates the possibility of traveling from the realm of the afterlife to the physical realm. Still, the Bible does make it clear that there is an existence of life beyond this lifetime, and the Jews who believe the Old Testament to be inspired by God believe in a life after death.

Some Jews believe that our ultimate goal is not getting to heaven but bringing heaven down to earth. To them, the real heaven is what happens down here as the fruit of the collective labor of the Jews throughout history. This sect of Jews believes the world will steadily improve until we usher in the messianic era. For obvious reasons, this is a little difficult to swallow.

More in line to Jewish thought is when the criminal on the cross asked Jesus to remember him and Jesus said, *"Today you will be with Me in Paradise"* (Luke 23:43 NKJV). Here we are given a picture into the Jewish understanding of an afterlife. There is a place called *pardes* in Aramaic or paradise in English.

What we need to do here is understand the Jewish language for the afterlife. Jews do not generally talk of heaven. Instead, they talk about *Gan Eden* or the garden of Eden, which is also known as paradise. This is where souls go while awaiting the resurrection and return to their corporeal life. The final phase or the eternal phase is *Olam Ha Ba* or the world to come—that is, the new world that God will repair and perfect. At this point, all souls will return to a corporeal body through a resurrection to experience the fruits of their labor. It is probably best to just follow their timeline:

1. Our current world: That is the here and now while I am writing this in this physical realm.

2. Garden of Eden: That is also now but in another dimension.

3. The Era of the Messiah: Also here, but not now.

4. Resurrection of the dead: The final stage of the messianic era.

5. World to come: Post-resurrection of the dead.

Those who are students of Bible prophecy will find this to be not that much different than what we believe. We live in this current world, but when we die we go to a place we call heaven and the Jews call the garden of Eden or paradise, which is a sort of retirement home for our souls while awaiting the next phase. The big difference is that the Jews believe the garden of Eden exists on this earth but in a parallel realm or universe. Many Jews believe that it is possible for those living in this realm of the garden of Eden to pass through and re-enter this world as Samuel did (see 1 Samuel 28:3–25); however, it is considered a painful experience for the departed. However, we are still on the same page as the Jews; once we pass from this physical body, our eternal souls will go to a place that we call heaven, and they call the garden of Eden.

Then there comes the era of the Messiah. We believe that started two thousand years ago with Jesus; the Jews are still expecting it to come. So, here our paths take a slight divergence, but we again dovetail in the next phase, which is the resurrection of the dead but then this splinters in different directions of eschatology. There are many views: premillennialism, postmillennialism, amillennialism, pre-tribulation, post-tribulation, and so on. There is a belief among Christians that there will be a seven-year tribulation period before the end of our messianic era. However, at the end of the seven years, we again dovetail into the Jewish belief of the era of the Messiah. They believe the era of the Messiah is a millennium period as we Christians call it, and this comes with the resurrection of the death. Then at the end of that there is the final phase where God will recreate the earth, the garden of Eden will return to the earth (or in Christian teaching, heaven will come down to earth), and we will enjoy an eternity in a new heaven and new earth.

So in a real sense, our view on heaven is not all that much different than the Jewish position. Ultimately, we will end with new incorruptible bodies to enjoy an eternity with God.

The most important thing I have learned from Judaism, however, is I am not serving God, tithing, going to church, and living a righteous life to earn a berth in heaven. As I live on this earth, I anticipate a home in heaven based upon the finished work of Jesus Christ and not any good works I do here. I am, however, focused on fulfilling my role, the mission God created me for here on earth.

30

THE INVERTED NUN

"When the ark set forward, that Moses said, Rise up, Lord, and let thine enemies be scattered; and let them that hate thee flee before thee. And when it rested, he said, Return, O Lord, unto the many thousands of Israel."
—Numbers 10:35–36

I have studied Hebrew under several different Christian Hebrew teachers in an academic environment. Then I studied Hebrew under rabbis, and I noticed a difference. Christian teachers treated Hebrew like any other language, while rabbis treated Hebrew like it was a holy language filled with many clues and hints to deeper understanding of a passage. For instance, some use the Gematria, which calculates the numerical value of a word. Each letter in Hebrew is also a number. Hence, every word bears a numerical value. *Yalad* is the Hebrew word for child. It is spelled with a *Yod*, which is also the number ten, a *Lamed*, which is the number thirty,

242 *What the Rabbis Know That I Never Learned in Church*

and a *Daleth*, which is the number four. If you add those numbers (10+30+4), the numerical value for the word "child" is forty-four.

The sages teach that when combining two totally different words creates the same value as another word, it indicates a relationship, giving you some deeper insight. So, let's take the word for "father," which is *av* spelled with an *Aleph*, which is the number 1, and *Beth*, which is the number 2. Adding them together is 1 + 2 = 3. The word for "mother" is *im* spelled with an *Aleph*, which is the number 1, and *Mem*, which is the number 40. Adding them together is 1 + 40 = 41. The numerical value of "father," which is 3, and the numerical value of "mother," which is 41, equals 44. Thus, you have a numerical relationship of 44 between a mother and a father, which produces a child, which has a numerical value of 44, which is the equivalent numerical value of a child.

Shared letters often suggest shared meanings. Sometimes a rabbi will rearrange letters. The word for grave is *kever*, which is spelled *Qop Beth Resh*. If you rearrange the letters, you could get *Beth Qop Resh* which is the word *boker* for morning. Here we learn that our final resting place, the *kever* or grave, is a *boker*, or morning to our next life.

In studying under rabbis, I found Hebrew taking on a new and exciting dimension. I had to pay close attention to details that Christian teachers tend to ignore. An example is a grammatical expression I never knew existed from my years of studying under Christian teachers, which is the *nun hafucha*.

This passage in Numbers is set off in the Sefer Torah with two specific symbols. They appear in some Hebrew texts as rectangles, "nuns," put together. It is called a *nun hafucha*. In English, we would call it an inverted nun. It is often overlooked by Christian Hebrew teachers because they consider it unimportant or are not even aware of it.

Some years ago, my study partner pointed out the inverted nun to me and asked what it meant. I really did not know so I decided to seek some understanding of this grammatical point. I discovered that the inverted nun does not appear in various Hebrew texts because it was considered an unimportant marking by the Hebrew scribes. Besides that, it is very difficult to express in type setting print and our fonts on a computer. Since it seems to be unimportant, it is just overlooked.

After my study partner pointed this out to me, I tried to recall my old Hebrew classes and if there was ever mention of the inverted nun or the *nun hafucha*. I tend to recall a couple of my Hebrew professors calling this simple accent mark, similar to other pointings and markings, without further explanation.

Maybe another reason the *nun hafucha* is not taught is because there is no real agreement as to what it means. However, if the most ancient text shows that inverted nun, then there must be an important reason behind it. Some liberal rabbis would say that it was an indication that the inspired nature of this text is in question. Other rabbis more generously say the inverted nun indicates that there is a question of the divine nature of these verses, and the nuns separate the verses to be questioned until Elijah returns to declare if these verses are inspired or not. Some feel the inverted nuns are used to indicate that this portion of Scripture is more important than others. Another theory (which I like, but it is not generally accepted) is that the nun is reversed to indicate that we are to consider the shadow of the nun. In Hebrews, Paul said that the journey in the wilderness was an example for us to not harden our hearts like the children of Israel (see Hebrews 3:7–19 and Hebrews 4:11). So as this was an example of faith, the reverse shows a lack of faith. Paul mentions that the story of the wilderness experience was given to us as a warning. We could learn from this that their faith scattered their enemies, and their lack of faith brought destruction (see Proverbs 1:27). I also like the idea that

244 *What the Rabbis Know That I Never Learned in Church*

the nun represents total devotion and the inverted nun shows the consequences of a lack of devotion.

The explanation that I lean toward, however, and feel most comfortable with is the more common explanation by esoteric Orthodox rabbis. Their explanation is that this passage of Scripture is to be moved to another position in Scripture after the Messiah returns. In this case, it is to be moved to a place after Numbers 17:2. It will then be in its proper place in Scripture. More mystical rabbis will say that the two inverted nuns form a roof or a completion—that the 85 words in Numbers 10:35–36 actually form a separate book. The Talmud teaches there are seven books to the Torah, not five. This would add another book, but it will not become a book until the Messiah returns. I am assuming the seventh book is the other place in Scripture where we find the inverted nuns and that is Psalm 107.

The fact that this creates a "floating" nature to Scripture—in other words the placement of a scripture verse can be moved by use of the inverted nun—would suggest that this is similar to what we in Christianity call "ongoing prophecy." Further explained, a word of prophecy in the Old Testament may have a fulfillment in the time it was written but will also point to a future event as well. That abomination of desolation is one such ongoing prophecy. It has had multiple fulfillments starting with Antiochus Epiphanes who offered up a pig on the sacred altar in 168 BC and desecrated the temple of God. There is also a future event called the abomination of desolation to take place in the future.

Here we have the teaching of an event that took place in history and the use of the inverted nun to show that there will yet be a similar event to occur in the future when the Messiah returns. As we believe the Messiah has come, we can claim this event over. Whenever the enemy approaches, and we are moving forward with the Lord as Israel moved forward carrying the ark with God's presence that now rests in us, thanks to the work of the Messiah Jesus, our enemies will arise and God will scatter the enemy. When we rest in the presence of God, He will return to us. The word "return" is *shuvah*, which could come from the root word *shuv*, which means to return. This, however, makes little sense in the context as God never left Israel when He scattered the enemy. For this reason, I believe the root word is *shavah* demonstrates another little glimpse into the depth of God's Word. In this case, this is a play on words meaning to take captive, which means God will not only arise and scatter our enemy, but He will take us captive. So long as we remain a captive or prisoner of God, the enemy need never touch us again.

31

EVANGELISM OLD TESTAMENT STYLE

"Yet now, if thou wilt forgive their sin—; and if not, blot me, I pray thee, out of thy book which thou hast written."
—Exodus 32:32

"For I could wish that myself were accursed from Christ for my brethren, my kinsmen according to the flesh."
—Romans 9:3

Jews do not practice soul winning. Yet the very nature of being Jewish is basically evangelistic. The Jewish understanding of being the chosen people is that they were chosen to bring to the world a knowledge of God Jehovah. Hence their confession, *"Hear, O Israel: The LORD our God is one"* (Deuteronomy 6:4). They have fought for over four thousand years to maintain a belief in just one God. The Maccabean war was fought as the first recorded war for ideological reasons, to maintain a monotheistic faith. In a sense, the Jews were our first evangelists.

248 *What the Rabbis Know That I Never Learned in Church*

I grew up in a fundamentalist Baptist church where soul winning was your ultimate job. I was told that if you would not confess Jesus before men, He would not confess you before His father.

Whosoever therefore shall confess me before men, him will I confess also before my Father which is in heaven. But whosoever shall deny me before men, him will I also deny before my Father which is in heaven. (Matthew 10:32–33)

The verse really says to, "deny Him before men, you will be denied before the Father." But I was just a kid and believed everything the preachers told me even if they misquoted Scripture. I never thought to fact check them at that time. However, to be denied by the Father was just as bad, if not worse. As a child I did not really understand what it meant, but I knew it was bad. I did not want to go to hell, and I was able to put together that Jesus not confessing or denying me to the Father was a sure way to end up there.

I was first told by the preachers that this meant you must go forward in church when the invitation was given at the end of a service. This was meant to make what they called a public confession or profession of your faith. I was never too sure which word applied as I heard both. If you were saved in your private time or alone you needed to make a public confession or your salvation was not yet certified. For a shy, backward little kid it took many days and weeks to build up the courage to walk forward in church. I figured from the preacher's sermons that my salvation was not yet complete until I made that public confession. With my courage intact, I went forward in church. Surprisingly, I found I had obtained instant celebrity status in our little church and the preacher even bragged in a sermon how I had received Jesus sitting in a school classroom. Had I known such honor was bestowed upon a public profession or confession I would have done so earlier with much more dramatic flair.

For a little while I felt I had achieved full salvation and was on my way to heaven when I hit another road hazard. I heard a preacher teach on evangelism and use those very same verses to apply to witnessing. He would point his finger at us and say, "Are you ashamed of Jesus?" I wanted to shout, "No," except he immediately followed that with, "If you do not witness or share the gospel with your friends and classmates at school, then why? Could the only reason be that you are ashamed of God?" Well, that was not really the reason for not sharing my faith. I was just too shy and scared. I was already the target of bullies and had very few friends. That would have been all I needed to do—start trying to evangelize my schoolmates. It was even worse that the popular cute girl, who seemed to always sit across from me in class, would never talk to me if I started to spout out religion. She never initiated a conversation over the twelve years of combined grammar and high school. I later learned, I don't know from what source, that her father was a Pentecostal preacher. So, I guess it was for the best that she was totally out of my league. I mean, after learning she was Pentecostal, I knew if by some miracle she did notice me, there would be no future in it. These Pentecostals spoke in tongues and my pastor said, "You stay away from that stuff. That tongues business is of the devil." I would sit across from her wondering if those demons would jump off on me. Yet, I had a hard time believing someone so cute, sweet, and adorable could be so bewitched by the demon stuff—speaking in tongues. However, those were the days when I believed everything that was spoken from the pulpit of our church was the inspired and inerrant Word of God.

I mean, this evangelism stuff was a lot to put on a shy little kid trying to impress his first romantic crush. Still, that didn't matter to the preachers who were trying to build their platform. That word "ashamed," I was told, meant that you were embarrassed to be associated with Jesus. I had now certainly reached the depths of despondency. If I was afraid and too shy to share Jesus with my schoolmates, then I truly was ashamed of Him. I knew my destination according to the preachers. I mean preachers and guest preachers tried every which way until Sunday to get people to come forward during an invitation. The more people responding to his invitation, the better his chances of getting asked to return for another guest spot. So what if you sacrificed a few vulnerable kids along the way? They would get over it. The only thing is, we don't get over it. We grow up to be biblical language teachers who do not trust anything we hear from a pulpit, and are in a constant state of fact-checking every preacher.

I lived through many fearful days thinking I would die and go to hell, or worse yet that the rapture would occur and I would be left behind. But this evangelism business was a tough nut to crack. I made some feeble attempts at it, failed miserably, and I still blush over the fool I made of myself. I wasn't sure how many witnesses you needed to qualify for salvation or even how many souls you needed to win. I figured there was a quota somewhere in heaven. God had assigned some angel to sit in the halls of records with a big quill pen and a visor keeping track of all our attempts to witness and record all the souls that we had won.

I had nightmares of dying and standing before the pearly gates where I was met by St. Peter who had a checklist. "Let's see, sinner's prayer? Check. Repentance with godly sorrow? Questionable. Baptism? Check. Regular church attendance? Check, with extra credit. Daily Bible study?

"Excuse me, I need to make a call to the executive office. Hey, Gabe, is 70% passing?

"Okay, no check. Daily prayer? Hmmm. A lot of give me and not much obligation. No check. Witnessing? Hoo boy, I need to make another call.

"Yes, outer darkness? Yep! Got another one for you. Yeah, trying to sneak in here claiming to be a good Baptist.'"

Many years later, after graduate school, I started to befriend rabbis and began studying their works. I mean, they are, after all, the chosen people and the people of the Bible. I discovered they were not interested in new recruits. In fact, they did everything they could to discourage people from converting. I never wanted to convert, but I sure envied their lack of evangelism. I often reflected how nice it would be to be part of a religion where you were not required to obtain converts.

Still, I was drawn to the teachings of Judaism. I was able to find a home for many of its teachings in my own Christian faith, which oddly enough made certain rabbis smile. As a good Baptist, you wanted rabbis to accept some of your teachings and convert, not apply those teachings to their Jewish faith. Although I got the distinct impression that there wasn't much in our Baptist faith that a rabbi would consider to be useful in his Jewish faith. Still, I ran across some teachings on evangelism in the Talmud and Midrash that gave me a whole new perspective on evangelism. After sharing it with you, I bet you might agree that it is something we evangelical Christians need to really embrace, particularly at this time in our history.

The Talmud and Midrash point out that, at first, there were no attempts at evangelism. The one most likely to evangelize would have been a fellow named Enoch. *"And Enoch walked with God: and he was not; for God took him"* (Genesis 5:24). He was the great-great-great-grandson of the first man, Adam. He walked with God, knew God personally, and devoted himself to Him. He was likely the only one on earth at the time, other than Noah, who was righteous. The rest of the world had abandoned God such that He would send a flood to destroy humankind. Jewish tradition teaches that Enoch was the seventh patriarch, and he lived in isolation because the world could have easily corrupted him. He was taken to heaven at the age of 365 years, while others lived to be 800–900 years. Living in isolation means he had no influence on the world, and he left this world without a convert. He never even prayed for the people.

As a child, that was my form of evangelism, which was none. I had no spiritual influence on any of my classmates, not even on my school crush. I was too terrified even to warn her of that demon stuff—speaking in tongues. I kept to myself, and maybe rightly so. I was so desperate for acceptance, I might easily have fallen into corruption. Had my crush noticed me and looked at me with those tender blue eyes, I would have started yakking away in tongues twenty years before I fell in with that gang. I never even bothered to pray for my schoolmates, although I did remember to pray for my crush.

Now along comes a man named Noah, the great-grandson of Adam, the tenth patriarch, who found grace in the eyes of the Lord. (See Genesis 5–9.) He obediently built an ark as God commanded him, and unlike great-grandpa Enoch, he did not hide himself away but was faithful to warn the people of the coming flood. He was not a successful evangelist, as his only converts were his own family. Noah's evangelism was only an obligation and the fulfillment of an obligation. There is no record he even prayed for the people.

Like Noah, by the time I made it into Bible college, I found I was obligated to evangelize. The first Bible college I attended was Calvary Bible College, where we were required to have a CSA (Christian Service Assignment). We could work around the evangelism part by working in an Awana program or being a Sunday school teacher. However, I was determined to rack up as many spiritual points as I could in evangelism. Although, by this time, I knew I did not have to be a soul winner to earn my green card into heaven, I still worried that I would get into heaven only *"so as by fire"* (1 Corinthians 3:15). That is by the *"skin of my teeth"* (Job 19:20). Not that I desired a big mansion or anything like that. A little one-room cabin by the lake would suit me just fine. But

I suffered enough humiliation growing up, and I didn't want to be that loser in heaven who kept getting bullied by the Christian elites. If I racked up enough evangelism points and maybe a soul here and there, I would at least be a normal heavenly citizen and not a charity case. So, I signed up to do door-to-door evangelism and lived in constant fear and distress that whole semester, facing that Thursday evening visitation team. I did it like Noah and ended up like Noah with no converts because I was doing it out of obligation. Like Noah, I never even prayed for the people we visited except as a group. I had to offer some prayer with the other students present so they wouldn't think I lacked compassion.

After the flood, there was a man named Abraham who came along. Now Abraham was our first evangelist. According to the Midrash, he set up a hostel and coffee house. Weary travelers would stop by for a good meal and a warm bed. When the people went to thank Abraham for his hospitality, Abraham would say, "Oh, don't thank me, thank God." The Midrash teaches that he worked to always put the name of God on the lips of the strangers he served. Abraham obtained many converts; he prayed for the people and showed he cared for the people and their needs. But still, he was only trying to promote the name of God as he felt obligated to do this. Although he did pray for the people, he really did not have to make any sacrifice for the sake of those he evangelized.

By the time I transferred to Moody Bible Institute, I was getting the hang of this evangelism stuff. I could avoid embarrassment by participating in Child Evangelism Fellowship, Awana, and the local rescue missions. Here, the sinners came to us, and I did not have to do any cold-calling evangelism. Child Evangelism Fellowship had an early release program from school as a way of demanding equal time as the Catholics who got out of school early every Wednesday for their Catechism class. We provided refreshments, games, Bible stories, and a presentation of *The Wordless Book* as our evangelistic tool. I had many converts. I cared about the kids

254 *What the Rabbis Know That I Never Learned in Church*

and had sympathy for them. I enjoyed giving them refreshments and a good time. I sincerely prayed for them as they were from economically disadvantaged and crime-ridden neighborhoods. But like Abraham, I still fell short of the ideal. You see there was no sacrifice on my part that demanded it. I traveled safely into the neighborhoods with a group, and we only worked during the day-time when it was safe. I was still fulfilling an obligation.

Finally, we reach the story of Moses who not only prayed for his people, pleaded with them to submit to God, but also declared, *"Yet now, if thou wilt forgive their sin–; and if not, blot me, I pray thee, out of thy book which thou hast written"* (Exodus 32:32). He cared so much for his people that he basically told God, "If You do not forgive these people, then You had better find Yourself another leader and just erase any record of me in Your Book of Life." What he said was, *"blot me, I pray thee, out of thy book."* The word in Hebrew for "blot" is *machah,* which means to wipe out, obliter-ate, or erase. To the Phoenicians, who were merchants, it was a word used to scratch out an item on a merchant's list so that it would not be included in the fulfillment of that order. The word "book" is *kathab,* and really means a record or a memorial. In other words, Moses is saying that if God wouldn't forgive these people, then don't forgive me, give me nothing, forget I even accepted this assignment, and give me no credit for anything.

Moses had the ultimate motive for his evangelism. It wasn't to earn heaven; it wasn't to earn any favor from God or even to enjoy demonstrating His power. He only cared about his people and that God forgave them. Paul had pretty much the same motive, *"For I could wish that myself were accursed from Christ for my breth-ren, my kinsmen according to the flesh"* (Romans 9:3). His desire for the salvation of his brethren and kinsman was so strong that he would be willing to be accursed from Christ. The word "accursed" is *charama* in Aramaic, which means to be separated from destruc-tion. Is Paul saying that he is willing to go to hell for the sake of his brethren? That is what separation from Jesus leading to destruction is. Many Bible scholars do not believe that is what Paul is saying. No one in their right mind would be willing to spend eternity in hell for another's sake. I believe Jesus would. Besides, to me, separation from Jesus for eternity is hell enough, and clearly that is what Paul is saying is that he is willing to be separated from Jesus for eternity if it would bring his brethren to salvation.

Ultimately, what he is saying is the same thing Moses said, "I want nothing from You, God, no rewards, no mansion in heaven, not even eternal life. What I want is to see my brethren saved." Such love can only come from Jesus Christ Himself. Would Jesus go to hell for eternity for us? I believe He would, simply because that is the only way Moses and Paul could have said what they said in all sincerity, which would be impossible unless they were motivated by the one capable of such love.

Well, I can't say I have reached that point. I would like to think I have at least reached the point of Abraham, but one thing I know is I will only share the gospel with someone if God puts that love and compassion in me to share His love. That means that I am not sharing the gospel with every Tom, Dick, and Harry coming down the pike. However, I do share the gospel many times, and it flows very naturally, for I am only responding to the motivation of God and the preparation of the Holy Spirit in the hearts of those I am sharing. Such evangelism will prove to be very successful.

What I learned from rabbis is that God is always on their lips. They just talk about God naturally because their lives revolve around God and His Word just like Abraham who cared for people and created a hostel and coffee house and asked for nothing in return other than they thank God Jehovah.

32

SARAH WAS A CONNECTION

"He hath made every thing beautiful in his time:
also he hath set the world in their heart,
so that no man can find out the work that
God maketh from the beginning to the end."
—Ecclesiastes 3:11

"He has made everything appropriate in its time.
He has also set eternity in their heart,
without the possibility that mankind will find
out the work which God has done from the
beginning even to the end."
—Ecclesiastes 3:11 (NASB)

"And it came to pass, when he was close to entering Egypt,
that he said to Sarai his wife, 'Indeed I know that you are a
woman of beautiful countenance.'"
—Genesis 12:11 (NKJV)

I must admit that when I read the NASB version of Ecclesiastes 3:11, which I was told was the closest translation to Hebrew, I was really disappointed. I grew up with the KJV and memorized all my Scripture verses in the KJV. The King James Version was the only version of the Bible allowed in our house. My younger brother, who is now a linguist with Wycliff Bible Translators, used to say as a toddler, "Can *ye* open the door?" So, I was adamant that the NASB was just plain wrong and had mistranslated what I read, *"He has made everything appropriate in its time."*

I loved that phrase, *"He hath made every thing beautiful in his time,"* and it seemed to me to be a real desecration of God's Word to exchange that beautiful word *"beautiful"* to *"appropriate."* Where were the hearts and souls of the linguists when they translated this verse? How could they render something so important about God's timing to something so mundane as appropriate? Yes sir, God will make everything adequate, decent, or acceptable in His time. That is how I viewed the word "appropriate." To me, to make everything beautiful meant it all turns out right and lovely. Birds are singing, flowers are blooming, and the aroma of grandma's biscuits—the best in the world—is in the air. That's what I think when I hear the word "beautiful." Use the word "appropriate," and I think not wearing my baseball cap in a sanctuary is *appropriate*. Saying certain words is not *appropriate*. I remember as a small child running in the aisle of the church after a service and being stopped by white-gloved ladies who would admonish me saying that it was not *appropriate* to run in God's house. Hence, I associate the word "appropriate" with the expected form of behavior. God is a strict, no-nonsense God, who does not tolerate behavior that is not appropriate. Ah, but that word "beautiful" conjured up pictures of peace, joy, and happiness.

Is the NASB wrong for using appropriate rather than beautiful? Well, let's just take a little linguistical journey with the word "beautiful". Beautiful is defined as, "having qualities of beauty, exciting aesthetic pleasure, and generally pleasing, and excellent."[9] So, what did King Solomon have in mind when he said that God will make everything beautiful in His time? Did he mean that God will bring everything to a high standard of excellence, as the NASB suggests? Did he mean that God will make everything pleasing to our senses in His time? Well, the word in Hebrew is *yaphah*, which means to be beautiful, to become beautiful.[10] The Brown-Driver-Briggs tells us it means fair and beautiful.[11] You sing it, BDB, and I'll hold the hymn book. But, of course, the *New America Standard Bible* says fitting or appropriate. In this, I take the stand of my father who used to say, "You can use those modern translations if you like, but for me I take the Bible." He said this as he held up his Scofield Reference King James Version.

But there are more roads to travel on our linguistical journey. First, let's examine the English word "beautiful." We use it in many different contexts. Someone will point to their new car and say, "Ain't she a beaut?" Why they always use the feminine pronoun may suggest why they refer to their car as beautiful. We associate beauty with feminine qualities. We don't say a man is beautiful; we say he is handsome. My dad was a fisherman, and he loved to fish. His most common expression when he pulled up a Muskie from the lake with its sharp, threatening teeth, and beady little eyes would be to declare, "Ain't she a beaut?" No, "she" wasn't a beaut! She (if it was a she) was slimy, ugly, slippery, slithery, greasy, mucky, clammy, and ready, willing, and able to bite my finger off. In the words of Margaret Hungerford, "Beauty is in eye of the beholder."

---

9. "Beautiful." Merriam-Webster.com Dictionary, Merriam-Webster, https://www.merriam-webster.com/dictionary/beautiful. Accessed 27 Nov. 2024.
10. Bible Hub. Strong's Hebrew. "Yaphah." https://biblehub.com/hebrew/3302.htm.
11. Bible Hub. Brown-Driver-Briggs. "Yaphah." https://biblehub.com/hebrew/3302.htm.

260　*What the Rabbis Know That I Never Learned in Church*

I recall when I was teaching, a student came to me after his wife gave birth to a little girl and proudly showed me a picture of this red, greasy, slippery, wrinkled form of a human being and, pointing to himself, declared, "Papa! Ain't she beautiful." I lied and said yes. Well, maybe not a real lie. In Judaism, a lie is when you say a falsehood to achieve selfish results at the expense of another person. All I did was confirm what my student passionately believed. I could have said, "I believe you believe she is beautiful." But I was a busy professor and did not have time for much more than a "yes."

In Genesis 12:11, Abraham tells his sixty-five-year-old wife that she is a beautiful woman, using the word *yaphah*. But then we all know that Abraham was a man of peace and peacemaking starts first in the home. But, hey, in the eyes of a husband who has loved his wife for over half a century, that woman is still beautiful.

I attended a high school with 5,000 students, and my crush was in many of my classes. As far as I was concerned, she was the most beautiful girl in the whole school. I lost track of her after graduation, but many years later, I found her social media profile that displayed a picture of herself and her husband. If I had not read on her profile of her faith and Christian walk with God, I might not have considered her so beautiful. However, to imagine her loving God, raising her children to love God, and having a loving husband who appreciated and loved her, made her appropriate to me. In God's timing, He made everything appropriate, right, and perfectly fitted for her.

So, as far as I am concerned, the KJV and the NASB are in agreement; they just use different words to express the same thing. In His time, He will make all things appropriate and beautiful. When something is appropriate, and fitted together perfectly, its beautiful. When you empty the box of a jigsaw puzzle, all those little pieces do not look beautiful, and they are not appropriate. But when you put that puzzle together and every piece is appropriately placed, you have a beautiful picture. So, too, in our lives with God. Our lives sometimes seem like a jigsaw puzzle—not too beautiful—but if you give God His proper time, He will put those pieces together where they fit and are appropriate, and the results will be beautiful.

When Abram and Sarai (we'll call her Sarah as that would be the name she is remembered by) entered Egypt, the Pharaoh found her to be attractive at sixty-five years of age and took her into his harem. Abram passed her off as his sister for fear the Pharaoh would kill him off to possess her. Well, no doubt Sarah could be beautiful at sixty-five years old.

Sarah, however, lived in a time when makeup and hair extensions were found only with royalty. Plus, she lived her life in a desert, and a desert is harsh on skin. A person growing up in a desert climate, facing the irritating elements of the desert, would look twice her age. Yet, we are led to believe that at the age of sixty-five, a king was head over heels for her, and later, when they encountered King Abimelech of Gera, she was pursued at the age of ninety.

I am not saying Sarah was not beautiful and desirable such that kings and princes would pursue her, but I cannot help but feel that these kings must have suffered from cataracts. Also, I do not question God's ability to perform a miracle and make Sarah more attractive and pleasing, but I think there is something more to it.

When I was working on my doctoral dissertation for my PhD in Archeology, I read something interesting. The Egyptian goddess Bastet, who was considered the daughter of Ra, was something like a mistress to the Pharaoh. It was believed that a sacred priestess dedicated to Bastet could transfer her powers through this priestess to a man who had a sexual relationship with her. In fact, many cults of goddesses, even the goddess Astarte, believed a goddess could transfer her powers through a human surrogate to a man through a sexual relationship. There are many variations to

262 *What the Rabbis Know That I Never Learned in Church*

this concept, and many archeologists suggest this is where the idea or concept of the virgin birth of Jesus came about, but I am not going to go there in this chapter.

What I find interesting is that this was not one visually challenged king who noticed the beauty or *yaphah* of Sarah, but his princes were the ones who reported her beauty to the king.

> *Therefore it shall come to pass, when the Egyptians shall see thee, that they shall say, This is his wife: and they will kill me, but they will save thee alive.* (Genesis 12:12)

Her beauty would have caught the eye of not just one nearsighted king, but all the men of Egypt. Now I am sure Abram and Sarah passed through many cities and towns that had kings and Sarah's *yapah* was never an issue there. Why, all of a sudden, was her beauty so profound that they would kill the woman's husband to possess her? There had to be something else in that mix, and I believe it was spiritual.

I found an answer to this question from Jewish literature and the way that the Jewish commentators handle the Hebrew. Note what Abraham says, *"Indeed I know that you are a woman of **beautiful countenance**"* (Genesis 12:11 NKJV). "Countenance" is the word *mare'eh* from the root word *ra'ah*. The word has the preposition *Mem* in front of it, so it is literally rendered "from seeing." *Ra'ah* could be both physical seeing and spiritual seeing. You can only tell which type from the context. Considering all the factors I have discussed, I would suggest this was a spiritual seeing or countenance. Sarah was a prophetess. Abraham was advised by God to listen to her in Genesis 21:12. Her words had the power of God. The kings all heard the stories about the God of Abraham and how God gave him great victories and power. You know how legends go. By the time they reached the Pharaoh, Abraham probably seemed like a man who could move mountains. This was a God who had powers that the King or Pharaoh would desire to tap into. How do you do it? The same way you get your power from the goddess. This would explain why the Pharaoh would kill Abraham if he were married to Sarah—to ensure he would be the sole possessor of this power from Sarah. Remove him and another man could get that power.

Note what happened when Pharaoh took Sarah into his home, "*And the* LORD *plagued Pharaoh and his house with great plagues because of Sarai Abram's wife*" (Genesis 12:17). In Hebrew, this is *al devar Sarai eshet Avram*. Translators tend to ignore the word *dava* and don't even translate it. Jewish commentators do not overlook this word. This should be rendered "because of the *words from the heart* of Sarai, Abram's wife." The word "plague" is the word *naga*, which means to touch. God touched the house of Pharaoh with great plagues with the words from Sarah's heart. *Naga* also means to be struck down or smitten. Pentecostals call it being slain in the spirit. Sarah spoke some words from the heart of God to her heart, and these words had such power that the Pharaoh and his house were struck down under the weight of the holiness of God. Note the word holiness is *kodesh*, which means weight.

Pharaoh knew he was up against something beyond his power and his gods. He was quite anxious to be rid of Abram and his wife. He would dare not kill him after such a demonstration of power from God, and he would be more inclined to enrich him, which is what he did.

As far as the beauty of Sarah goes, that word *yaphah*, according to Jewish Hebrew scholars, could also mean a connection. I believe the attraction was not so much her beauty but also her *yaphah*, her connection with God. They were able to discern something different spiritually about her. King Abimelech most likely had the same designs on Sarah in chapter twenty where God revealed to him in a dream the horrible things that would befall him. He knew Sarah had a connection with a very powerful God, and he desired that connection.

We today can have the same connection with God through an intimate relationship with Jesus Christ. Sarah and Abraham knew how to tap into that connection with God. We learn in the New Testament that it was through faith that Abraham was able to please God and tap into that connection with God. It was the same with Paul, who was bitten by a poisonous snake but tapped into that relationship with God and did not die. As a result, all the sailors who were with him were amazed and listened to his instructions after that. (See Acts 28:1–6.)

Days are coming and are here where we believers in God Jehovah will also be tapping into that connection with God and will speak words that will cause people to fall and call upon the name of God to be delivered.

33

GOOD WINE

"Jesus saith unto her, Woman what have I to do with thee?
mine hour is not yet come."
—John 2:4

As discussed in an earlier chapter, in the King James Version rendering of this verse, it sounds like Jesus was being very harsh, rude, and disrespectful to His mother. The Aramaic language gives us some perspective on this. John was a Galilean fisherman, so Aramaic would have been his native language. Hence the Syriac version of the Bible would carry a better understanding of the word *"woman"* that is used here. The word rendered as "woman" is *'anath* in Aramaic, and the Greek rendering, which is *gunai* seems to be in agreement. He was addressing his mother as a married woman. *'Anath* is a married woman or a woman who is not a virgin, and the Greek is simply a married woman.

One would have to ask, would not simply saying the Aramaic word for "mother," which is *'amah*, accomplished the same thing

266 *What the Rabbis Know That I Never Learned in Church*

and been more respectful? Well, not really. The Aramaic word, *'amah*, is cognate to the Hebrew word *'alamah*, which means an unmarried woman. It is often a reference to a young girl. A young girl would not be married but there are also references to adult, mature women who were also unmarried. It is rare to have an adult woman who is unmarried unless she is a widow. In some cases, it might refer to a woman who was divorced or abandoned. The Hebrew word *'alamah* is the same word used in Isaiah 7:14, which was a double prophecy and speaks of an *'alamah* or virgin who will conceive and bear a son. There would be a fulfillment in Ahaz's time as a sign that his enemies would be destroyed by God, as well as a future event of a coming Messiah who would be born of a virgin. The word *alamah* was an excellent choice of words for this prophecy as it could mean both a virgin and non-virgin. The term would be used for a non-virgin but an unmarried woman who bore a son during Ahaz's time and a virgin, Mary, who bore the Messiah.

Perhaps in this story in Matthew where Jesus calls His mother "woman," Jesus was making a little play on words hinting at a little secret shared only between He and His mother. At that time, He was the Son of God in fulfillment of Isaiah 7:14 and maybe He would do a little miracle to set the stage for His entry into His messianic mission.

On the other hand, calling His mother *'anath* in Aramaic was really a sign of respect in that culture. Joseph would have most likely died at this point but not before Mary had other children and would thus no longer be a virgin. In a sense, Jesus was doing her an honor, calling her an *'anath*, as this would be declaring that she was a single mother, by the death of her husband, who raised her children under the hardship of widowhood. I have heard successful men and women speak with pride for their mothers when they say, "My mother was a single mother and raised me." I think the NIV, which did a little paraphrasing, expressed it best—*"Dear woman."*

The expression *"mine hour is not yet come"* is really an Aramaic idiom. The BYOB concept was a common practice at Middle Eastern weddings with every male bringing his own brew and trying to show off that he had the best wine. Maybe the other women were starting to give Mary a hard time that her son did not bring any wine to the wedding as was the custom. Mary may have been keeping a little secret that her son was going to offer the best wine ever. Jesus's response to His mother in Aramaic was literally, "what to you and to me, not yet woman." We could interpret that phrase, based upon the context, as something almost conspiratorial, "What we talked about, dear woman, but not yet—patience." With a little knowing and maybe the smugness of a proud mother, she went to the attendants and instructed them to do whatever Jesus said. She knew what Jesus proposed to do would be a bit strange, and she had to prepare the servants. Jesus was going to use the water in the vessels that the guests used to wash their hands and feet before the meal. When He ordered the servants to fill the vessels, He was saying to add water to replace the water splashed out during the bathing. Keep in mind that people did not wash their hands and feet for hygienic purposes in those days; they did it for ritualistic purposes, as required by Jewish law to symbolize purification or cleansing. Jesus was going to demonstrate His role as the Messiah by taking the filth and dirt and purifying it.

Still, people washing their hands and feet after traveling through dusty roads can make the water rancid. That is probably why Jesus waited until the last hour to introduce His BYOB. It was culturally accepted and a sign of good hospitality for guests to get inebriated at a wedding. Jesus was probably waiting until the guests were too drunk to care if they were drinking bath water or not. I suspect John recorded this story to declare to the world and future generations that Jesus came to this world to take all its grimy, stinking, filthy sins, and purify it into pure good wine.

I found something interested in the Mishnah, which is a commentary of Jewish law. I have always been taught as a Baptist that the wine Jesus made at this wedding feast was just grape juice and had no alcohol in it. I do not drink alcohol of any kind, not for religious reasons, just because I was raised to not drink any alcohol. However, to be fair, I highly question that the wine Jesus turned the water into was just grape juice. The Mishnah clearly defines the number of days that wine was to be fermented for various occasions. Fermentation is the conversion of grape sugars into alcohol and carbon dioxide by yeast. This process can take a few days to several weeks. This depends upon several factors, including grape variety, yeast strain, and temperature. Wine used in a wedding had to be fermented for three to four days. This would have yielded a low to moderate alcohol content based upon the climate of the Middle East. Good wine in those days among the Jews was wine that was used for ceremonial purposes. The good wine served at this wedding had an alcohol content, contrary to what I was taught growing up as a Baptist.

34

HOSANNAH

*"And the multitudes that went before, and that followed,
cried, saying, Hosanna to the Son of David:
Blessed is he that cometh in the name of the Lord;
Hosanna in the highest."*
—Matthew 21:9

*"Save now, I beseech thee, O LORD: O LORD,
I beseech thee, send now prosperity."*
—Psalm 118:25

On Palm Sunday, we celebrate the triumphal entry of Jesus in Jerusalem. Many people gathered palm branches to wave and lay before Jesus as He rode into Jerusalem on a donkey. We call this Palm Sunday as that was one distinction of that day, and everyone at church gets a palm branch. The reason the people brought out the palm branches was because they were expecting another deliverance. The palm branches had also been used during the celebration of the liberation of the Jews by the Maccabees in the second century BCE (1 Maccabees 13:51) that is commemorated during the Jewish holiday of Hanukkah.

> *Rejoice greatly, O daughter of Zion; shout, O daughter of Jerusalem: behold, thy King cometh unto thee: he is just, and having salvation; lowly, and riding upon an ass, and upon a colt the foal of an ass.* (Zechariah 9:9)

Actually, it would be more accurate to call it "Donkey Sunday" and everyone gets a little plastic donkey, as the donkey was what was really predicted in Scripture. However, I doubt it would carry the same flair as Palm Sunday. Besides some adolescents (or adolescents at heart) would want to stretch their liberties and decency by using ass rather than donkey.

There was something else predicted in Zechariah 9:9, the King arriving with salvation. The fame of Jesus had spread throughout Judea and people began to talk. Rumors started that this was the Messiah, and He was heading for Jerusalem. Like all prophetic people, they began to spread the rumor that this was the fulfillment of Zechariah 9:9, and He would arrive on a donkey to declare salvation (this might have been started by the chief priest). Most people equated salvation with deliverance from the Roman Empire. They would not have been the first prophetic people to mix up the prophetic signs.

Unlike what we are usually taught, they did not turn against Jesus a week later. They were just quickly silenced like a political supporter of an unpopular candidate. They had cancel culture in those days as well. The court area of those who cried, "Crucify Him!" was filled with paid agitators, egged on by the chief priest and his supporters. The court where Pilate stood was small, and the only people who were allowed to enter were those approved by the chief priest. Mel Gibson's movie *The Passion of the Christ* had it right, showing guards turning the true supporters of Jesus away.

Hosannah 271

It was what we call today a kangaroo court. The Jews hated capital punishment as described in an earlier chapter, and the Talmud is filled with so many legal obstructions to the laws of capital punishment that it became virtually impossible to execute someone under Jewish law. Hence the high priest and Sanhedrin found it easier to bring Jesus before a Roman court rather than a religious court to have him tried for the crime of treason. This would make the death penalty much easier to acquire, and the triumphal entry proved to be perfect evidence of treason. I wouldn't put it past the chief priest to have staged the whole triumphal entry to build a case of treason against Jesus and ironically use the people's adoration of Him to do it.

Most incriminating evidence came not only from the palm branches reflecting liberation but also from the shout of Hosanna. You probably learned from your preacher or priest that Hosanna is a proclamation of praise. That is confusing Hosanna with Hallelujah, although colloquially it can mean praise. But to the first century Jews, it meant something else. Bible scholars believe the word was taken from Psalm 118:25 and people were quoting this psalm. The first word is *hoshi'ah* which means save now. This comes from the root word *yasha'* where the name *yeshua*, Joshua or Jesus, comes from. It means salvation. However, to the mind of the first-century Jew, salvation did not indicate a spiritual matter but a political matter. All throughout the Old Testament, it talks of being saved and salvation, and we Christians simply relate it to being born again when, in the mind of the writer, it meant deliverance from a foreign enemy.

This word *yasha'* in Aramaic is in an Ethtaphal form, which makes it causative and means to be delivered, rescued, or saved. Hence it means "do something to bring about our deliverance." The word is in an imperfect form and could read as "you will deliver us" or, as most translators believe as I do, that the *Hei* at the end is a paragogic *Hei*, which is an intensifier, thus, "Save or deliver us now." The word is really a compound word: *yehsaha* and *anna*. *Anna* comes from the root word *ani* or *anah*, which means to answer or respond. It can be taken as a plea expressing a strong desire for an answer as "please respond."

Put together Hosanna would translate out as "Please answer our prayer for deliverance." Of course, "Save us now" also works.

35

WHERE GOD DWELLS

"And Abraham called the name of that place Jehovahjireh: as it is said to this day, In the mount where the LORD is seen."
—Genesis 22:14

"And Isaac went out to meditate in the field at the eventide: and he lifted up his eyes, and saw, and, behold, the camels were coming."
—Genesis 24:63

"And this stone, which I have set for a pillar, shall be God's house: and of all that thou shalt give me I will surely give the tenth unto thee."
—Genesis 28:22

Let me share with you something interesting that I found when I was studying the Talmud. I was reading in Pesachim 88a. Jacob calls the place where he met God the *House of God*. Not like

Abraham who called it a mountain (see Genesis 22:14); not like Isaac, with whom it is called a field (see Genesis 24:63); but like Jacob, who called it a house (see Genesis 28:19). The Talmud went on to explain that it was on the mountain that God was *seen* (*ra'ah*, meaning in the Spirit) by Abraham. A mountain is a place that is visited at certain times. Isaac met God in a field, a place where you meditate with God on occasion, but it is not a permanent home. Jacob called this place where he met God on a rock on top of a mountain, known today as Mt. Moriah or Mt. Zion, God's house. The rock where he laid his head and had his dream of a ladder extending from the mountain to heaven is the same rock that the holy of holies in the temple was built around and where the ark of the covenant containing the very presence of God rested in a *tzim tzum* bubble. He laid his head on that rock, his head which contained his brain, which carried his consciousness, which contained his soul and heart. When he called this the house of God, he was referring to the soul, his heart. As Paul said, *"Know ye not that your body is the temple of the Holy Ghost"* (1 Corinthians 6:19). *"Know ye not"* in Aramaic is *lo yada'ain 'anathon*. The word know—*yada'in*—is in a *Pael* form as an active participle. In other words, this is something the Jews have always believed, from the time of Jacob, that God dwells within our bodies, which is why we must live a righteous life so that He may manifest Himself through us to the rest of the world. This is literally saying that God's home is not just the temple, not just that church building, but it is in our hearts. We talk of dying and going home to heaven. Yet, if heaven is where God dwells, then we are already home.

Today, many of us attend a church where we see God in the Spirit through worship, praise, and the imparting of His Word. But then we come home, have dinner, turn on the ball game, and go about our business. Before we go to bed or when we start our new day, we will have a short time of Bible study, prayer, and meditation on God. Then we will go to work and face the trials of the day. Do we leave God behind when we leave the church building or our quiet place of meditation, prayer, and Bible study? Of course not. God goes right to work with us and faces the trials of the day with us. Because of life's duties and daily cares, we cannot always be thinking of God. We cannot always be in church. We do not live in church.

Some time ago, I went through a period of darkness or what St. John of the Cross called the "dark night of the soul." It was during this time that I learned that God is not just my *mountain, my field,* but He is also *my home.* The word for "mountain" in Hebrew is *harar. Harar* is also the word for thinking. People often went to the mountains to be closer to God and to think and meditate on God. A pregnant woman in Hebrew is *harah,* which is the word mountain in a feminine form. A pregnant woman was believed to be closer to God for she carried God's creation of life in her.

The word field is *sadeh,* which is also the word for nourishment and produce. We spend time in meditation on God's Word to be nourished spiritually so we can go out and produce something for the Lord.

How many of us, however, see God as our home? The word in Hebrew for "house" or "home" is *bayith,* which means a dwelling place. It is where you abide and where we are 24/7 with God. We cannot worship God on a mountain 24/7 or meditate on Him in a field 24/7, but we can abide with Him 24/7. He is with us wherever we go. When we die, everything about us will change except for one thing: we will still be with God.

I was thinking about how my parents loved God all their lives. God was their home. At an elderly age, they one day fell into a state of unconsciousness, and within a few days, their bodies began to shut down, and then they passed on. Everyone said that they went home. They did not *go* home. They were always home; they just moved their residence to continue being with Jesus.

276 *What the Rabbis Know That I Never Learned in Church*

My father used to tell me the story of a young man in his outfit in the army during WWII. His name was Benny. Benny grew up on a farm in the country. His whole life was on that little farm with his mother, father, sister, and little brother. That was, until one day he found himself in that foreign, alien environment known as the US Army.

Benny was a good soldier. Having grown up in the country, he was in top physical condition; he was a natural sharpshooter, having spent his life hunting wild game to help feed his family. Benny was a good soldier except for one thing—he was homesick. He would walk around the base with my father and say, "Floyd, I miss my family, my mother, father, sister, little brother. I just have to go home." My father would try to encourage Benny and tell him: "Benny, just hang in there; in a few weeks, you will finish basic training, and you will get a leave to visit your family." But Benny couldn't wait, and sure enough, one morning, when there was roll call and Benny's name was called, there was no answer. Benny had gone home.

It didn't take the army long to find Benny and bring him back. For whatever reason, Benny was not severely punished. Maybe it was because he was such a good soldier with a near-perfect record, that and possibly his commanding office also had a family and longed for home as well. Nonetheless, Benny was allowed to rejoin his outfit and finish basic training. One night, after lights out, my father went to Benny and asked, "Benny, did you make it? Did you make it home?" When my father asked that question, Benny's face lit up as he said, "You know, Floyd, when I crossed that last hill, I looked down, and there I saw our little house, smoke coming from the chimney. I knew my mother and sister were preparing dinner, and I saw my father and little brother in the field mending a fence. My little brother, he was the first to see me on that hill. When he did, he dropped everything and started to jump up and down shouting, 'Dad, it's Benny! Benny's a come home, Benny's a come home.' My father and brother left that field as I left that hill, and I came to my house, my home, where they all greeted me."

Then my father always concluded the story by saying that he told Benny it was just too bad he had to return to the army. But Benny said, "I am still home, for my family is with me in my heart, and one day, when this old war is finished, I will return to my home, my home to stay."

As I have learned from my Jewish teachers, in my heart, I am home now; my God is in my heart. I may still be in the field and on that hill or mountain, but in my heart, I am home, and one day, when I cross that last hill, I will be home to stay.

36

THE HEART OF GOD

"The LORD is on my side; I will not fear:
what can man do unto me?"
—Psalm 118:6

"I know that the Lord is always on the side of the right.
But it is my constant anxiety and prayer that I and this
nation be on the Lord's side."
—Abraham Lincoln[12]

Abraham Lincoln, if he did indeed say the above words (I believe enough historical evidence exists to say he did), pointed out a very real problem with the KJV rendering of Psalm 118:6. Can we be so bold as to say that the Almighty is on our side?

I have been on a journey of over twenty years, searching for the heart of God. This book reflects much of that journey for it was

---

12. Abraham Lincoln Quotes. "God and Prayer." https://www.abrahamlincoln.
org/features/speeches-writings/abraham-lincoln-quotes/index.html#gap

280 *What the Rabbis Know That I Never Learned in Church*

through rabbinical teachings that I gained much of my knowledge regarding the heart of God.

The literal rendering for Psalms 118:6 is, "The LORD is for me." The word translated "*for me*" is spelled *Lamed Yod* and is a combination of the preposition *Lamed* (to or for) and the pronoun *Yod* (me). Some translations will render this as, "*The LORD is with me.*" However, the preposition *Lamed* is normally rendered as to, for, or unto, but it can be rendered as with; however, that is not its normal use. I believe the preposition "for" is the most accurate. To say the Lord is "*with*" me or "*on my side*" is not necessarily saying the Lord is "*for me.*"

David is not just saying the Lord is on his side or with Him; he is saying the Lord is *for* him. In other words, when opposing influences come into play, the Lord is the only one that is *for* him. All other influences have a personal agenda. God has no other agenda than to love us.

I believe the rest of this verse will bear this out. The remaining part of this verse says, "*I will not fear: what can man do unto me?*" The word "*do*" is *ashah*, which means to perform a work. In our culture, if someone performs a work for us, they usually expect something in return, some form of payment. The word "*fear*" or *yara'* in Hebrew is a complicated word. It does not necessarily have to have the idea of fear for one's safety, but more often is used for fear of the wellbeing of another.

I believe therein lies the message of Psalm 118:6. When David is saying that he does not fear any *work* that man can do for him, he is saying that when man does any *work* for him, he is under obligation to these people, but if the Lord does any work for us, we have no obligation to Him in return. After all, He is the creator of all things, the Almighty, the Omnipotent. What do we have that He could possibly want that He cannot get for Himself unless we give it to Him? The only thing we can give Him that He cannot get for Himself is our love. If our relationship with God is not a love relationship, then we are continually serving Him either out of a sense of repayment for a debt or to obtain something like eternal life. However, if we truly love Him, we will freely accept whatever work He does for us without a feeling of debt, knowing that He is doing it out of love. Our response to Him will be out of love and not out of obligation. This, I believe, is the true context of Matthew 10:8, "*freely ye have received, freely give.*" You have received from God without any obligation to Him; thus, we are to freely give without anyone feeling obligated to us.

Therefore, when we do give to God in return, it is with a pure heart and that will please Him more than any tithe, offering, or sacrifice. If we tithe with one hand and a greasy palm extended with the other hand, is that a true expression of love? Are we really seeking to know God's heart or are we focused on our own needs and wants?

One of my favorite rabbinic stories sums up the most important contribution to my personal Christian faith that I received from the works of rabbis. It is a story about a king who had two daughters. One was very selfish and self-centered. The other was a very loving and caring young woman. One day the selfish daughter marched into the throne room and demanded that her father, the king, hire the best seamstress in the kingdom to make a dress for her for an upcoming event. Without hesitation, the king, the father, snapped his fingers and ordered a servant to get it done. That evening during dinner, the other daughter, the loving, caring daughter, came to her father and said, "I have heard you hired the best seamstress in the kingdom to make a dress for my sister for an upcoming event. I, too, plan to attend this event. Could she make a dress for me?" The king, this father, motioned for his daughter to sit down. He ordered a plate of food for her and they began to talk, as a father and daughter would talk. The king, this father, took great joy in hearing of his daughter's life and struggles and took even greater joy in offering fatherly advice. Before long, the

282 *What the Rabbis Know That I Never Learned in Church*

dinner ended, and the king had to return to his duties. As he stood up to go, this loving daughter asked if she could have the dress. Her father said he would think about it. The next evening, this loving daughter came to him again with the same request. Again she shared dinner with her father, and again, they talked as only a father and daughter would talk. At the close of the dinner, she again asked for the dress, and again, the father said he was still thinking about it. This went on for the next few days, each time the daughter sharing dinner with her father, asking for the dress, and each time her father saying he was thinking about it. After a few days, a servant came to the king with a question, "Master, we in your court have a question we would like you to answer. You have this selfish, self-centered daughter who asked for a new dress, and you give it to her without hesitation. Yet, this loving, caring young child comes to you with the same request, and you keep putting her off, why?" The king, this father, just sort of stared off into space and said, "I am afraid that if I give her what she wants, she will not have dinner with me again."

We may be like that loving daughter. We may go to our heavenly Father with a request day after day, having dinner with Him and bringing up our request. Yet He seems to never get around to answering our prayer. Perhaps we need to pause, look beyond our request, and see what is in our heavenly Father's heart.

In my thinking, the major difference between Judaism and Western Christianity I have found is that we in the Western world seem to embrace our Christian faith for what we can get from it. We seek prosperity, healings, and solutions to our problems, not to mention a heavenly home. In Judaism, the goal is to love the Lord our God with all our hearts, soul, and might.

I have not converted to Judaism. I am a Christian and a gentile, but I also recognize that my Christian faith was birthed through Judaic teaching, and somewhere within our Christian faith, we have lost the perspective that God is not a celestial genie who grants wishes. He is a loving heavenly Father who only wants to be a part of our lives.

ABOUT THE AUTHOR

Chaim Bentorah teaches biblical Hebrew, Aramaic, and Greek to lay teachers and pastors in the metro Chicago area through Chaim Bentorah Ministries. He also speaks to church and parachurch groups about the nature and means of studying the Old Testament in the original Hebrew. His books combine a devotional emphasis with scriptural studies into the deeper meanings of Hebrew words.

Chaim and his study partner, Laura Bertone, write daily word studies on their blog at www.chaimbentorah.com. They are also the copastors of a cyber Messianic church through their subscription All Access online at HebrewWordStudy.com, on which they conduct twelve-week classes in basic Hebrew, a weekly Monday evening Bible translation class, and a Sabbath Torah study on Saturday mornings that follows the Parshah (Weekly Torah Portion).

Chaim has a bachelor of arts degree in Jewish Studies from Moody Bible Institute, a master's degree in Old Testament and Hebrew from Denver Seminary, and a PhD in Biblical

Archaeology. All of his Hebrew professors in college and graduate school were involved in the translation of the New International Version of the Bible. In their classes, he learned of the inner workings involved in the translation process. In graduate school, he and another student studied advanced Hebrew under Dr. Earl S. Kalland, who was on the executive committee for the translation work of the New International Version. It was this committee that made the final decisions on the particular renderings used in the original NIV translation.

Having done his undergraduate work in Jewish Studies, Chaim was interested in the role of Jewish literature in biblical translation. Professor Kalland encouraged him to seek out an orthodox rabbi and discuss the translation process from a Jewish perspective. From this experience, he discovered many things about the Hebrew language that he had not learned in his years of Hebrew studies in a Christian environment. Later, from his contact with Jewish rabbis and his studies in the Talmud, the Mishnah, and other works of Jewish literature, as well as his studies in the Semitic languages, Chaim began doing Hebrew word studies as devotionals and sending them out by e-mail to former students whom he had taught in his thirteen years as an instructor in Hebrew and Old Testament at World Harvest Bible College, as well as those he taught through Chaim Bentorah Ministries.

In addition to several self-published books, Chaim is the author of *Hebrew Word Study: Revealing the Heart of God*; *Hebrew Word Study: Exploring the Mind of God*; and *Journey into Silence: Transformation Through Contemplation, Wonder, and Worship*. Chaim co-authored *Hebrew versus Greek: A Devotional Study of Scripture Through Two Lenses*.

Welcome to Our House!
We Have a Special Gift for You

It is our privilege and pleasure to share in your love of Christian books. We are committed to bringing you authors and books that feed, challenge, and enrich your faith.

To show our appreciation, we invite you to sign up to receive a specially selected **Reader Appreciation Gift**, with our compliments. Just go to the Web address at the bottom of this page.

God bless you as you seek a deeper walk with Him!

WE HAVE A GIFT FOR YOU. VISIT:

whpub.me/nonfictionthx

Whitaker House